**DATE DUE**

| | | | |
|---|---|---|---|
| MAY 8 '7 | | | |
| MAY 29 '7 | | | |
| NOV 0 6 '7 | | | |
| FEB 1 8 '7 | | | |
| MAR 17 '7 | | | |
| DEC 9 '8 | | | |
| FEB 2 '83 | | | |
| MAR 6 '83 | | | |
| APR 1 '9 | | | |
| | | | |
| | | | |
| | | | |

☆

The years from 1800 to 1815 were an era of dramatic growth—and growing pains—for the young American nation.

In 1800, most Americans lived the life of forest pioneers, field farmers, or country craftsmen. But by 1815, urbanization was on its way as the "dark satanic mills" of textile factories and gun shops spread across New England.

During this period Americans mastered the sea and pushed westward on land. But as they crossed the continent, they began to oppress and destroy the Indians who stood in their path. They had rid themselves of British domination during the Revolution, yet in 1812 they began a second bloody conflict with England. The people believed in every man's right to "life, liberty and the pursuit of happiness," and Thomas Jefferson dreamed of a land free of slavery. Yet during his Presidency, slavery grew by leaps and bounds.

Here is a vivid picture of the American experience in a time when contradictions were expressed not only in the lives of the ordinary people, but also in the personal conflicts of their leaders.

*The Living History Library* series, under the general editorship of John Anthony Scott, provides a fresh, human and challenging approach to the study of the American past. Its overall theme as a series is the history of the United States as told by the people who shaped it. In each book, songs, documents, letters, and diaries are joined by a sustaining commentary to illuminate a given facet or topic in the history of the American people.

*The Living History Library*
*General Editor:·John Anthony Scott*

# FOR JEFFERSON AND LIBERTY

## The United States in War and Peace

# 1800-1815

## Leonard Falkner

*Illustrated with maps and contemporary prints*

ALFRED A. KNOPF  :  NEW YORK

## To Lisa, Christina
## and Jimmy

☆

THIS IS A BORZOI BOOK PUBLISHED BY ALFRED A. KNOPF, INC.

Copyright © 1972 by Leonard Falkner

Library of Congress Cataloging in Publication Data

Falkner, Leonard.
    For Jefferson and liberty.

(The Living history library)
    SUMMARY: A history of the United States during the Jefferson era illustrated with contemporary prints, paintings, and cartoons.
    1. Jefferson, Thomas, Pres. U.S., 1743–1826
—Juvenile literature.  2. U.S.—History—1801–1809
—Juvenile literature.  3. U.S.—History—1809–1817
—Juvenile literature.  [1. U.S.—History—1801–1809.  2. U.S.—History—1809–1817.  3. Jefferson, Thomas, Pres. U.S., 1743–1826]
I. Title.
E332.79.F3        973.4′6        71–168993

ISBN 0-394-82047-9
ISBN 0-394-92047-3 (lib. bdg.)

Manufactured in the United States of America

Grateful acknowledgment is extended to the following for permission to reprint copyrighted material:

Farrar, Straus & Giroux, Inc.: *Slave Songs of the Georgia Sea Islands* by Lydia Parrish. Copyright 1942.

W. J. Gage: *Canada's Story in Song* by Fowke, Mills and Blume.

E. J. Grassmann: *Under Their Vine and Fig Tree: Travels through America 1797–99, 1805* by Julian Niemcewicz. (Elizabeth, N.J.: for the New Jersey Historical Society, 1965, translated and edited by Metchie J. E. Budka).

Harcourt Brace Jovanovich, Inc.: *The American Songbag* by Carl Sandburg. Copyright 1927.

# CONTENTS

☆

FOR JEFFERSON
AND LIBERTY

☆| 〔 |☆

# AMERICA IN 1800

In 1800 comparatively few people crossed the Atlantic unless they had to. The dangers of the open sea were considerable, the journey long and uncomfortable. Nevertheless, the merchantmen plowing the seas between Europe and America carried some share of gentlemen travelers in addition to the usual complement of diplomats, businessmen, and landless immigrants.

One such traveler was Isaac Weld, a young Irishman of twenty-two who shipped out from Dublin aboard a square-rigged merchantman in 1795. Accompanied by his man-servant and a supply of quill pens, India ink, and sketch-books—the equivalent of today's camera—Isaac Weld was ready and eager to "establish the truth of various accounts of the flourishing and happy condition of the United States of America."

It had been a hard crossing. The fifty-nine days at sea, he recorded, "were disagreeable in the extreme, calms and heavy adverse gales retarding our progress westward." Now he stood on the deck of the ship, watching the coastline come into view, and with it, a sight that had all but disappeared from the shoreline of western Europe—virgin timberland stretching down to the ocean and extending as far as one could see.

*The first objects which meet the eye on approaching the American coast are the tops of trees which thickly cover the shore to the water's edge. At last the tall forest rising out of the ocean presents itself in all its majesty.*

This first impression—of a primeval wilderness—was recorded over and over again in the writings of travelers sighting America at the end of the eighteenth century. A ship beating up the coast from Georgia to Maine in 1800 could sail for days past landscapes still unknown to white men. It was a vast, rough, and largely unknown country that confronted the travelers of the time, and Weld may have suspected even then that his adversities at sea would be good training for the months ahead.

More than curiosity motivated the young man. The son of a prominent Dublin family (and named after his grandfather's good friend, Isaac Newton), he had little in common with the immigrants who might have been sickening in the hold of the very same ship— except for one factor: the search for a possible haven. Ireland, encouraged by the American Revolution, was in rebellion against the British overlords who had ruled there for centuries. "Storms are gathering over my native country," Weld wrote in his journal. The outcome was doubtful, and he wanted, "in case of emergency, to learn whether those [United States] might be looked forward to as an eligible and agreeable place of abode."

A generation earlier the Continent, and especially France, would have seemed the proper place for a young Irishman of good family to make his way. But Europe was in a state of upheaval. In 1789, a revolution in France had disrupted the ancient social system and touched off a war that threatened to engulf all the European nations, from Spain in the West to Russia in the East.

For close to a decade, the French Republic had been locked in combat with England and other monarchies, who were ready to tolerate a republic across the sea, but not in the heart of Europe. Under the brilliant leadership of Napoleon Bonaparte, a Corsican-born general scarcely over thirty, France was on her way to becoming the greatest land power in the west. By 1800, however, she was a republic in name only, for Bonaparte had made himself dictator in the closing months of the eighteenth century.

With the fleets of England and France vying for the upper hand, hostilities continued on the high seas as well as on land—often at the expense of neutral shipping. An American ship might find its cargo confiscated by either side or part of its crew impressed into service on a British man-of-war.

Weld's ship docked at Philadelphia, then the capital of the United States. Compared with the crowded, bustling market towns of the British Isles, America's second largest town (population 40,000) wore a serenity and tidiness that pleased the young traveler.

"The streets are tolerably well paved," he observed, "with pebblestones in the middle and on each side a footway paved with red brick." The houses themselves were mostly of brick, small and compact, flush against the sidewalks. "While there are few great houses to compare with those of our manorial lords back home,

*A wedding party painted by an unknown
American artist.*

neither are the homes of the humble as mean." Workmen's pay was much better in America than in the Old World, since land was plentiful and a man could go forth on his own if dissatisfied with his employment.

One of the rare displays of official pomp he saw was the president, portly John Adams, taking his daily outing in an enameled and gilded state carriage drawn by four matched horses, with a coachman and attendants in satin liveries. In contrast, a tall horseman in plain clothes and a limp tricorn hat cantering down Market Street one morning was pointed out to him as "Mr. Thomas Jefferson, our vice president."

To Weld's European taste, the homes on tree-shaded Chestnut and Walnut streets were old-fashioned. The furniture recalled the taste of an earlier day—solid and comfortable, but already discarded back home for lighter and daintier styles. The fireplaces were larger than Weld was accustomed to, since they burned wood from the surrounding forests of hickory and oak instead of the grate coal used in the British Isles. A strange fragrance filled the living rooms after dark. The lighting, as at home, was furnished by candles set in wall sconces and chandeliers, but here the candles were bayberry, made from the fruit of the wax myrtle that grew wild in the fields nearby.

Soon Mr. Weld and his manservant were off to see what the rest of the country was like. He planned first to visit the South and then return to Philadelphia to catch a stagecoach west.

In the first year of that new century, the United

States was still primarily a seaboard nation, hemmed in between the Atlantic on the east and the mighty Appalachians on the west. To be sure, wagon trains of pioneers had already worn two trails across the hundred-mile barrier of the Allegheny range in the central Appalachians. Of the three new states in the Union—Vermont, Kentucky, and Tennessee—two lay west of the mountains. Nevertheless, in an underpopulated country of barely over five million inhabitants, where the roads were few and poor and where commerce depended on waterways, the focus of national life was still in the original thirteen states at the eastern edge of the continent.

The republic in those years extended down to the troubled border between Georgia and Spanish Florida, but Weld confined his southern tour to Maryland and Virginia. Given the transportation of the time, even a stage coach trip from Philadelphia to Baltimore was a hardship. Except for the post roads that linked Boston to New York and New York to Philadelphia and Baltimore, there were practically no highways. Even the post roads were often no more than wagon ruts cut through the forests, as Weld soon discovered, jouncing on the Baltimore stage.

*The roads were so bad that the driver frequently had to call to the passengers to lean out of the carriage, first at one side, then the other, to prevent it from oversetting in the deep ruts. "Now, gentlemen, to the right," on which the passengers all stretched their bodies half way out of the carriage to balance it on that side. "Now gentlemen, to the left," and so on.*

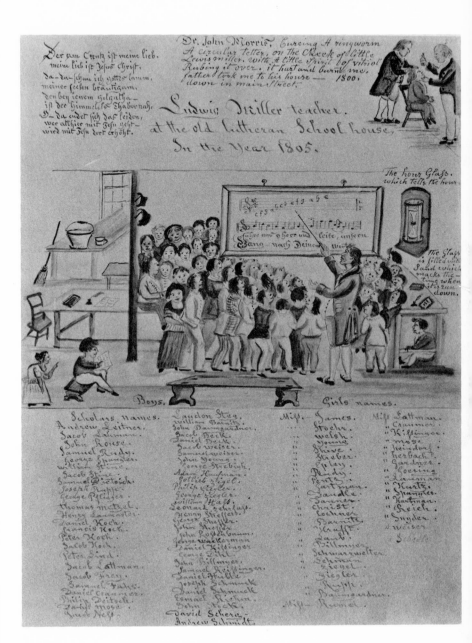

*Early American school scene by Lewis Miller, 1805.*

The stagecoaches offered little comfort. They were open, flat-bottomed vehicles without springs, drawn by two or four horses, depending on the condition of the road. There were seats for twelve passengers, but the driver was seldom averse to crowding aboard a few more. "To guard against bad weather," Weld noted, "there are curtains made to let down from the roof and fasten to buttons on the outside."

Isolation and primitive accommodations added to the discomforts of the trip. Only five of the nation's towns —New York, Philadelphia, Boston, Charlestown in South Carolina, and Baltimore—numbered more than ten thousand inhabitants each. Of the 5,308,483 Americans counted in the census of 1800, fewer than 200,000 were city folk. The rest—farmers, plantation owners and their slaves, village shopkeepers, rural craftsmen, woodsmen—lived scattered over a vast area of fields, forests, mountains, and swamplands. Under the circumstances, the overland traveler must take such overnight lodgings as he could find. Unhappily for Weld, the New York-Baltimore run was no exception to the general dismaying rule.

*Every ten or twelve miles on this road, there are taverns built of wood, only distinguishable from other houses by the number of handbills pasted to the walls near the door. The accommodations are very indifferent. Those who travel through the country must often submit to be crammed into rooms where there is scarcely space to walk between the beds.*

*At Elkton my first inquiry of the landlord on alight-*

ing, as there were many passengers in the stage, was to know what accommodations his house afforded. He seemed surprised that any inquiry should be made on such a subject and told me I need not give myself trouble, as he had no less than eleven beds in one of his rooms.

Sleeping in the same bed with his servant was a new experience for Weld, but he soon discovered that two to a bed was the best that could be hoped for in these lonely taverns. At times the stage passengers had to sleep three and four together. Everything, in fact, seemed to be handled on a mass basis.

At each house there are regular hours for breakfast, dinner, and supper, and if a passenger arrives beforehand it is vain to ask for a meal for himself. He must wait for the appointed hour and then sit down with the other guests. For breakfast there is tea and coffee, bread, cold salt meat, beef steaks, and fried fish.

On inclement days the passengers followed a morning ritual to supplement the scant protection of the stagecoach. "Before they pursued their journey," Weld wrote, "they took hearty draughts of egg-nog composed of milk, eggs, rum and sugar."

The stage line ended at Baltimore, where Weld found "the streets not all paved, so when it rains heavily they are almost impassable. The great number of houses are of brick but in general small, heavy and inconvenient." Baltimore, smallest of the American cities (population 13,000), left the young Dubliner singularly unimpressed.

In order to proceed south from Baltimore, Weld

bought a horse and sulky. His goal was the new capital of the United States. Forty miles to the south, amid a wilderness of forest, swampland, hills, and ravines bordering the Potomac, a new townsite was being laboriously constructed. It would be called Washington, after the first president. Weld soon found that the roads leading to Washington were atrocious.

*Between the hills are patches of black earth called bottoms. After a heavy rain the wheels sunk up to the very box of my sulky in one of these. For a moment I despaired of being about to get out. But my horse, which was very powerful, threw himself on his haunches, disengaged his fore legs and made a vigorous plunge which disengaged both him and the sulky.*

At the next tavern, Weld learned that General Washington, traveling north from Mount Vernon, had once been stopped in the same place, "his carriage sinking so deep in the mud that it was necessary to send to a neighbor's house for ropes and poles to extricate him."

Fording the rivers in winter proved equally rugged. Weld found the Susquehanna partly frozen over. "A number of travelers desirous of getting across" huddled on the shore, while the crewmen, Negro slaves, made the flat-bottomed ferryboat ready.

*The passengers were about twelve in number with four horses. The boat's crew consisted of seven blacks, three of whom, with large clubs, stood upon the bow of the boat and broke the ice, while the others with iron-*

*High Street Market, Philadelphia, in 1800,*
*by William Birch.*

headed poles pushed the boat forward. So very laborious was the task which the men at the bow had to perform, that it was necessary for the others to relieve them every ten minutes. At the end of half an hour their hands, arms, faces and hats were glazed entirely over with a thick coat of ice.

Viewing Washington, D.C., in its then primitive state, Weld agreed heartily with those Americans who objected to President Washington's selection, ten years before, of this remote site for the capital city.

Those people maintain that it can never become a town of any importance, that all those who think to the contrary have been led astray by a few enthusiastic persons. They assert the people to the eastward will never submit to a seat of government removed so far from them.

The president's house, its interior still unfinished, was "two stories high and built of freestone," as noted by Weld, who added, "it is undoubtedly the handsomest building in the country, but many persons find fault with it as being too large and too splendid for the residence of any one person in a republican country."

Weld and his manservant put up at Tunicliffe's, the town's only tavern, long enough to ease their travel aches before resuming the journey south. Their course followed the eastern bank of the Potomac, through country that in earlier days had provided rich tobacco harvests for its colonial settlers. But tobacco plants have a robust appetite, and repeated planting had long ago exhausted the soil. The settlers had moved on, leaving a man-made wasteland behind.

*The country wears a most dreary aspect. Nothing is to be seen here for miles together but extensive plains that have been worn out by the culture of tobacco, overgrown now with a wild grass called sedge and interspersed with groves of pine and cedar trees, the dark color of which forms a curious contrast with the yellow of the sedge.*

The travelers found the remains of "several good houses," mute witnesses of a better time.

*These were the houses, most probably, of people who originally settled in Maryland with Lord Baltimore, but which have now been suffered to go to decay, as the land around them is worn out, and the people find it more to their interest to remove to another part of the country, and clear a piece of rich land, than to attempt to reclaim these exhausted plains.*

They stopped at a tavern. It was, Weld noted,

*one of those old dilapidated mansions that formerly was the residence of some wealthy planter, and at the time when the fields yielded their rich crops of tobacco would have afforded some refreshment to the weary traveler; but in the state I found it was a picture of wretchedness and poverty. . . . As for the poor slaves, however, of which there were many in the huts adjoining the tavern, they had a most wretched appearance, and seemed* to be half starved. The men and women were covered with rags, and the children were running around stark naked.

Back home in Dublin, whenever the talk turned to the American Revolution, the town most often mentioned was Williamsburg, the colonial capital of Virginia. There the first seeds of rebellion had been nourished to full flower by a little group of brilliant men, among them George Washington, Thomas Jefferson, and Patrick Henry. But after the war the capital had been moved to Richmond, and the Williamsburg Mr. Weld saw no longer wore the splendor of its colonial days.

*Williamsburg is going to ruin. Numbers of the houses at present are uninhabited, evidently on account of its inland situation with no navigable streams near it. Richmond, on the contrary, has increased very fast because it stands on a large navigable river.*

Here the young traveler made an observation that explains why some early American towns would remain small—places such as Deerfield and Stockbridge in Massachusetts, Staunton in Virginia, Frederick in Maryland—while others would grow. Western expansion was already building up eastern cities.

*The size of all towns is proportionate to their trade with the back settlements, supplying the people of the western parts of the United States with articles of foreign manufacture; hardware, woolen cloths, figured cotton, hosiery, haberdashery, earthenware, etc, from Eng-*

land; coffee and sugar from the West Indies; and tea, coarse muslins and calicoes from the East Indies.

Seeing work gangs of black men and women in the fields, a mounted white overseer riding herd on them, was a new experience for Weld. Here in the lush interior of Virginia, thanks to their black work forces, *the principal planters have nearly everything they can want on their own estates. Amongst the slaves are found tailors, shoemakers, carpenters, smiths, turners, wheelwrights, weavers, tanners, etc. I have seen patterns of excellent coarse woolen cloth made in the country by slaves, and a variety of cotton manufactures, among the rest good nankeen* [a durable fabric made originally from Chinese cotton]. *Cotton grows here extremely well.*

*The large estates are managed by stewards and overseers, the proprietors just amusing themselves with seeing what is going forward. The work is done wholly by slaves, whose number are in this part of the country more than double that of white persons.*

Weld apparently had ample opportunity to observe the life of the slaves on the more benevolent sort of plantation.

*Their quarters, the name whereby their habitations are called, are often situated one or two hundred yards from the dwelling house, which gives the appearance of a village to the residence of every planter in Virginia. . . . Adjoining their little habitations, the slaves commonly have small gardens and yards for poultry, which are all their own property. They may have ample time to at-*

*A New England mail stage.*

tend to their own concerns, and their gardens are generally found well stocked and their flocks of poultry numerous. Besides the food they raise for themselves, they are allowed liberal rations of salted pork and Indian corn. Many of their little huts are comfortably furnished and they are themselves in general extremely well clothed. In short, their condition is by no means so wretched as might be imagined.

But the visitor found it hard to reconcile the bondage of the blacks with their masters' lip service to the rights of man.

Still, however, let the condition of a slave be made ever so comfortable, as long as he is conscious of being the property of another man, who has it in his power to dispose of him according to the dictates of caprice; as long as he hears people around him talking of the blessings of liberty, and considers that he is in a state of bondage, it is not to be supposed that he can feel equally happy with the freeman. It is immaterial under what form slavery presents itself, whenever it appears there is ample cause for humanity to weep at the sight and to lament that men can be found so forgetful of their own situation as to live regardless of the feelings of their fellow creatures.

While the blacks slaved, Weld reported, their white overlords idled most of their time away at the gaming tables. Throughout southern Virginia and parts of Maryland, Weld found a billiard room in almost every tavern, "and this is always full of a set of idle fellows, drinking spirits or playing cards, if not engaged at the table."

The southern tavern was also the scene of cockfighting, a favorite diversion among the lower classes.

"The circumstance of having the taverns thus infected by such a set of people renders traveling extremely unpleasant," Weld complained. "Many times I have been forced to proceed much farther in a day than I have wished, in order to avoid the scenes of rioting and quarreling that I have met with at the taverns."

To the young man from overseas, the sounds and sights in the foliage and skies above him offered a welcome contrast to the sordidness of the isolated taverns. In the constant bird concert overhead, Weld heard no single voice that he thought matched that of the nightingale or skylark back home, but he found the voices pleasing when combined and the birds themselves "superior in point of plumage." Farther south he saw his first vultures and noted an early example of ecology legislation.

*In the lower parts of Virginia, and to the southward, are great numbers of large birds, called turkey buzzards, which when mounted aloft on the wing look like eagles. In Carolina there is a law prohibiting the killing of these birds, as they feed upon putrid carcasses, and therefore contribute to keep the air wholesome.*

Turning westward from Richmond through the rolling, plantation-scattered countryside reaching to the Blue Ridge Mountains, Weld found fertile country

*Susquehanna River scene.*

producing abundant crops. To harvest those crops, however, the planters had to contend with the heavy rains that often washed the seeds—and sometimes the crops themselves—out of the clayey soil.

*After heavy torrents of rain I have frequently seen all the Negroes in a farm dispatched with hoes and spades to different fields, to be ready to turn the course of the water, in case it should take an improper direction.*

"Notwithstanding the utmost precautions," erosion was taking place in these fertile foothills, settled but a half-century before.

*On the sides of the mountain, where the ground has been worn out with the culture of tobacco, and left waste, and the water has been suffered to run in the same channel for a length of time, it is surprising to see the depth of the ravines or gullies, as they are called, which it has formed.*

Weld had now arrived at the village of Charlottesville, set among fat, tree-crested hills rising to the Blue Ridge skyline. The neighborhood had a distinguished citizen in Thomas Jefferson, the vice president whom Weld had seen cantering down Market Street in Philadelphia. Mr. Jefferson was still occupied with his duties in the nation's capital, but his plantation's open-handed hospitality to travelers was not curtailed by his absence. The young gentleman from abroad was promptly given a comfortable bed—a most welcome change—and wholesome food; his linen was washed, his boots polished.

In consequence, we have the earliest description of Monticello, the classic hilltop mansion wholly designed by Jefferson.

*It is most singularly situated, being built upon the top of a small mountain, the apex of which has been cut off, so as to leave an area of about an acre and a half. At present it is in an unfinished state; it will be one of the most elegant private habitations in the United States. A large apartment is laid out for a library and museum, meant to extend the entire breadth of the house, the windows of which are to open into an extensive green house and aviary. In the center is another spacious apartment, of an octagon form, reaching from the front to the rear of the house, the large folding glass doors of which, at each end, open under a portico. . . . The mountain whereon the house stands is thickly wooded on one side, and walks are carried around it, with different degrees of obliquity, running into each other. On the fourth side is the garden and a large vineyard that produce abundant fine fruit.*

It was hard to believe that this had been frontier a little over two generations ago. Now the frontier lay beyond the mountains, and to penetrate that country, Weld had to return north to Philadelphia. From there it meant yet another jaw-rattling stagecoach ride—this time west across the Allegheny Divide to Pittsburgh, the busy gateway to the Ohio River Valley. The young man may have been a little limp by this time, his curiosity somewhat dampened by the rigors of the road. Except for the food in the mountain taverns—wild pigeon, buffalo and bear meat, and coffee made of roasted dried peas—he had little new to recount.

Another foreign visitor of the day made the journey alone, on horseback. He was Thomas Ashe, a retired British soldier and world traveler. Perhaps Mr. Ashe was simply a hardy soul, or possibly the steep stagecoach fare of $20 lay beyond his means, as he had recently been released from a French prison, after serving time for wounding a Frenchman in a duel. Certainly few travelers cared to brave the Allegheny barrier alone. But whatever his reasons may have been, Ashe's trip enabled him to leave a record of the richness of natural life that still prevailed in the eastern mountains in 1800. After one night alone in the hills, however, Ashe made sure that he ended his day's travel, if not at a tavern, at least in some settler's cabin.

*Darkness brought the din of the demons of the wood. Clouds of owls rose out of the valleys and flitted screaming about my head. The wolves, their howling reverberating from mountain to mountain, held some prey in chase, probably a deer. Nor was the panther [probably a wildcat] idle. One was employed close by me, and like our little domestic creatures of the same species, delighted in tormenting his victim. He had caught an opossum, as I understood by its lamentations, but was in no haste to kill it. The intervals between these cries and roarings were filled by the noise of millions of other little beings.*

Commonest of those "other little beings" were the

passenger pigeons, now extinct, but so plentiful then that they weighed down the trees at night and in flight could turn midday into eerie twilight.

One didn't have to go to the plains to find buffalo. Ashe's circuitous journey brought him to a region of salt springs to which the buffalo, "having a great fondness for salt," had for ages past beaten a trail through the wilderness.

*An old man, one of the first settlers, had built his log house on the immediate border of the spring. One day soon thereafter the buffalo came, traveling in droves of about 300 each. So unacquainted were these poor brutes with the nature of this man's house that they in a few hours rubbed the house completely down. He had difficulty to escape being tramped under their feet or crushed to death in the ruin of his house.*

On the other side of those lonely mountains lay the great river valley that opened westward toward the Mississippi and the center of the continent. To the northwest were the territories of Ohio and Indiana; to the southwest, the new states of Kentucky and Tennessee. By 1800 more than 250,000 settlers traveling mountain and river routes had cleared new homesteads in the valleys of the Ohio, Cumberland, and Tennessee rivers, their stump-pocked cornfields and pumpkin patches obliterating the ancient hunting grounds of the Shawnee and Iroquois.

The key to these lands was Pittsburgh, thriving at the eastern end of the Ohio. The Pittsburgh that Weld and Ashe saw had grown in twenty-five years from a log outpost of the French and Indian War to a town of some four hundred houses, many of which, according to Ashe, were "large and elegantly built of brick." Ashe also counted "forty stores, differing from our shops at home in being larger and dealing in everything that can be expected to be asked for."

These general stores did a lively business supplying the pioneers from across the mountains for the final leg of their journey by water to new homesites farther downstream. Another busy institution was the horse auction. Here many of the immigrants sold the teams and wagons that had taken them across the mountains and bought flatboats to carry their possessions the rest of the way into the wilderness.

Winter in the robust little riverbank town, Mr. Ashe discovered, was anything but dull.

*Carioling or sleighing predominate. The snow no sooner falls than pleasure, bustle and confusion banish business, speculation and strife. Nothing is seen but mirth. All the young men of a certain condition provide themselves with handsome carioles and good horses, and take out their favorite female friends, whom with much dexterity they drive through the streets, calling on every acquaintance and taking refreshments at many open houses.*

Conviviality often continued at night, when the merrymakers would meet "at a tavern several miles distant to which they go by torchlight and accompanied by music. On arriving, the ladies cast off their fur pelisses and with the men commence the mazy dance."

## Young Charlotte (*The Frozen Girl*)

This song has been popular since pioneer days in all parts of the country where piercing winter cold meant an ever-present danger of death by freezing. Different melodies were used in different places; the one given here is from Indiana. The lyrics are from Ohio.

Young Char - lotte lived on a moun - tain side in a
And yet, on man - y a win - ter's eve young

wild and lone - ly spot. There
swains were gath - ered there, For her

were no dwell - ings for three miles wide ex -
fa - ther kept a soc - ial board, and

cept     her   fa  -  ther's     cot.
she     was   ve  -  ry          fair.

2. On New Year's Eve the sun went down,
    Far looked her wistful eye
Out from the frosty window pane,
    As the merry sleighs dash by.
At the village fifteen miles away
    Was to be a ball that night,
And though the air was piercing cold,
    Her heart was warm and light.

3. How brightly beamed her laughing eye,
    As a well-known voice she heard,
And, dashing up to the cottage door,
    Her lover's sleigh appeared.
"Oh daughter dear," the mother cried,
    "This blanket round you fold,
For 'tis a dreadful night abroad,
    You will get your death of cold."

4. "Oh nay, oh nay," young Charlotte cried,
    As she laughed like a gypsy queen,
"To ride in blankets muffled up,
    I never would be seen.
My silken coat is quite enough,
    You know 'tis lined throughout,
And there is my silken scarf to twine
    My head and neck about."

5. Her bonnet and her gloves were on,
     She jumped into the sleigh,
   And swift they sped down the mountain side,
     And over the hills away.
   With muffled beat so silently,
     Five miles at length were passed,
   When Charles with few and shivering words
     The silence broke at last.

6. "Such a dreadful night I never saw,
     My rein I scarce can hold;"
   Young Charlotte faintly then replied,
     "I am exceeding cold."
   He cracked his whip, he urged his steed,
     much faster than before,
   And thus five other weary miles
     In silence were passed o'er.

7. Spoke Charles, "How fast the freezing ice
     Is gathering on my brow!"
   And Charlotte still more faintly said,
     "I'm growing warmer now!"
   Thus on they rode through the frosty air,
     And the glittering cold starlight,
   Until at last the village lamps
     And the ballroom came in sight.

8. They reached the door and Charles sprang out,
     And held his hand to her;
   "Why sit you like a monument
     That hath no power to stir?"
   He called her once, he called her twice,
     She answered not a word,
   He asked her for her hand again,
     But still she never stirred.

9. He took her hand in his, 'twas cold
     And hard as any stone;

He tore the mantle from her face,
  As the cold stars o'er it shone.
Then quickly to the lighted hall
  Her lifeless form he bore;
Young Charlotte's eyes had closed for aye,
  Her voice was heard no more.

10. And there he sat down by her side,
  While bitter tears did flow,
And cried, "My own, my charming bride,
  You never more shall know."
He twined his arms around her neck,
  He kissed her marble brow,
And his thoughts flew back to where she said,
  "I'm growing warmer now."

Thomas Ashe may have enjoyed his stay, but the serious-minded Isaac Weld caught the first available flatboat bound down the Ohio and Mississippi to the Spanish port of New Orleans. These two great rivers were the highroads to market for the frontiersmen, since it was impossible to transport their crops across the mountains. The 2,100-mile journey took Weld only twenty-eight days. For settlers to pole or row back upstream, he learned, took as much as three months. On reaching New Orleans, therefore, they would sell their boats for the worth of the lumber, board a ship sailing up the eastern seaboard, and return home across the mountains by stagecoach.

It was all too primitive, too different from anything Isaac Weld had ever known. The tidy charm of Philadelphia, the beauty of the plantation country, the elegance of Monticello, could not erase the impression left by the months of stagecoach riding, flatboat travel, primitive inns with their rough company and indifferent food. Weld made his way back north as quickly as he could, passing through New York and Boston, and going on to Canada. From Quebec he sailed home in 1797, "entertaining not the slightest wish to revisit the American continent."

## ☆ 2 ☆

# A BEGINNING AND AN END

Weehawken in 1804 was a strip of green perched atop the Palisades—the lava cliffs rising from the New Jersey edge of the Hudson River. It was quiet, isolated, yet accessible by water, and therefore a suitable dueling ground for hotheads ferrying across the river from Manhattan Island on the New York side.

On July 11, 1804, the duelists who leveled their pistols at each other were no less than the vice president of the United States, Colonel Aaron Burr, and the former secretary of the treasury and Federalist party leader, General Alexander Hamilton. New York City's *Morning Chronicle* described the encounter:

*Col. Burr arrived first on the ground, as had been previously agreed. When General Hamilton arrived the parties exchanged salutations, and the seconds proceeded to make their arrangements. They measured the distance, ten full paces, and cast lots for the choice of position, as also to determine by whom the word should be given, both of which fell to the second of Gen. Hamilton. They then proceeded to load the pistols in each other's presence, after which the parties took their stations. The gentleman who was to give the word then explained to the parties the rules which were to govern them in firing. . . .*

*He then asked if they were prepared; being answered in the affirmative, he gave the word "present," as had been agreed on, and both parties presented and fired in succession; the intervening time is not expressed, as the seconds do not precisely agree on that point. The fire of Col. Burr took effect, and Gen Hamilton almost instantly fell. Col. Burr then advanced toward General Hamilton, with a manner and gesture that appeared to General Hamilton's friend to be expressive of regret, but without speaking, turned about and withdrew, being urged from the field by his friend, as has been subsequently stated, with a view to prevent his being recognized by the surgeon and bargemen who were then approaching. No further communication took place between the principals, and the barge that carried Col. Burr immediately returned to the city.*

Hamilton lay dying. His friends took him by boat to a house on Jane Street in Greenwich Village. It was a tiny community lying amid the green fields north of New York City. There he remained for two days, until death put an end to his agony.

This duel brought to a dramatic close the fierce enmities generated by the disputed election of 1800. This election had made Thomas Jefferson president and Aaron Burr vice president. It had also ended the twelve-year rule of the Federalists, a coalition of merchants and planters, lawyers and clergy that had ruled the United States since 1789 and whose most brilliant leader had been Alexander Hamilton.

The Federalist party had made a great contribution to the welfare of the young republic. Their best leaders, like George Washington and Hamilton, had headed the revolutionary struggle against England. They had conceived and created the Constitution of 1788 and had secured its adoption in the teeth of bitter anti-Federalist opposition. They had organized the first national government under the new Constitution. But now, in 1800, this powerful party was falling apart. The reasons were to be found in the policies which they had pursued since 1789—the levying of unpopular taxes, the use of the army to suppress popular protest, and the passage of laws to stifle dissent.

The opposition to the Federalists crystallized during the 1790s around the leadership of Thomas Jefferson, whom a British diplomat described as

*a tall man, with a very red freckled face, and gray neglected hair; his manners good-natured, frank, and rather friendly, though he had somewhat of a cynical expression of countenance. He wore a blue coat, a thick gray-colored hairy waistcoat, with a red under-waistcoat lapped over it, green velveteen breeches with pearl buttons, yarn stockings, and slippers down at the heels— his appearance being very much like that of a tall, large-boned farmer.*

Jefferson's unassuming appearance fitted well with his image as "a man of the people." Jefferson, by 1800, had made himself a spokesman for farmers, craftsmen, shopkeepers, city dwellers, and frontiersmen. He stood for friendship with revolutionary France rather than monarchist Great Britain, the splendor of country living

*Political rivalry in Congress, a 1798 cartoon.*

*Federalist anti-Jefferson cartoon.*

rather than the sordidness of the city, the rights of the people rather than the power of government.

In the election of 1800, Jefferson needed the city vote, but he personally had little use for the growing urban centers of the new nations. As American minister to

AND ON THIS.

HERE IS _____

_____ like a mildewd ear,
Blasting his wholesome brother _____

*Vide Hamlet.*

York, June, 1807.

France, he had seen enough misery in the squalid cities of the Old World. "While we have land to labor," he wrote,

*let us never wish to see our citizens occupied at a work-*

*bench or twirling a distaff. Carpenters, masons, smiths are wanted in husbandry; but for the general operation of manufacture let our workshops remain in Europe. The mobs of great cities add just so much to the support of pure government as sores do to the strength of the human body.*

Ironically, it was the voters of New York City and Philadephia, well organized by men like Aaron Burr, who handed the much-needed electoral votes of New York State and Pennsylvania to Thomas Jefferson. Aaron Burr was a member of a distinguished New England family, a veteran of the Revolutionary War, and a former U.S. senator. He ranked with Alexander Hamilton as one of the most able lawyers in the nation's leading commercial community. These two men, interestingly enough, were not only rivals in politics and law, but also in finance. Hamilton was a director of the important Bank of New York, while Burr had founded the Bank of Manhattan.

But there was one important difference between the two men. In 1800 Burr was at the pinnacle of his fortune; Hamilton's successes all lay behind him. Hamilton could look back on brilliant services to the Revolution as an artillery officer and as aide to Washington. His great commentary on the Constitution in the *Federalist Papers* had helped procure the ratification of that instrument; and until 1795, he had been the dominant figure in Washington's administration. In that year personal scandal put an end to his public career, and he returned to the obscurity of private law practice in New York City.

In the fall of 1800, Americans went to the polls in unprecedented numbers, although property requirements still existed in most states. Of the five candidates for office, four were under party labels—Jefferson and Burr for the Republicans, Adams and Charles Cotesworth Pinckney for the Federalists. The Republican party caucus had clearly designated Jefferson as the presidential candidate, but Republican party unity demanded that the electors support Burr equally, even at the risk of incurring a tie that would throw the election into the House of Representatives. It was not until 1804, with the passage of the Twelfth Amendment, that each elector was obliged to vote separately for the president and vice president and thus prevent a tie vote between two candidates of the same party.

The election was a wild and hilarious affair, as the voters swept to the polls to vote against the Federalists and to put on record their stored-up resentments against the party in power. "Jefferson and Liberty" was a campaign song that made its first appearance during this election, and it remains one of the most popular campaign songs of American history. It celebrated the simple virtues of Jeffersonian philosophy, elation at the approaching end of Federalist rule, and boundless confidence in the nation's destiny as a free and democratic republic. The great vision of the American dream was set to the tune of an Irish jig with a majestic sweep all of its own.

# Jefferson and Liberty

The gloom-y night be-fore us flies, The
reign of ter-ror now is o'er; Its
gags, in-quis-i-tors and spies, Its
herds of Har-pies are no more.

**CHORUS**
Re-joice, Co-lum-bia's sons, re-joice; To
ty-rants nev-er bend the knee; But
join with heart, and soul and voice, For
Jef-fer-son and lib-er-ty.

No lordling here with gorging jaws
Shall wring from industry the food,
Nor fiery bigot's holy laws
Lay waste our fields and streets in blood!
*Chorus*

Here strangers from a thousand shores
Compelled by tyranny to roam,
Shall find, amidst abundant stores
A nobler and a happier home.
*Chorus*

Here Art shall lift her laurel'd head,
Wealth, Industry, and Peace divine;
And where dark, pathless forests spread,
Rich fields and lofty cities shine.
*Chorus*

Not all the people of the country, of course, shared these sentiments. Some looked upon the possibility of Jefferson's election as a catastrophe which the country would not be able to survive. A handbill distributed in New England warned electors against Jeffersonian designs.

*They call themselves the friends of the people and Mr. Jefferson the man of the people. Beware of such an assumed title! The object with him is the same as with the French leaders. They wish to destroy a government which controls them and set up one by which they can control others. The leading Republicans in this country are among the most despotic of our inhabitants!*

Under the cumbersome system set up by the Constitution, the voters in each state elected a group of electors equal in number "to the whole number of senators and representatives to which the state may be entitled in Congress." This group of electors, known as the electoral college, then assembled in each state; each elector was entitled to cast two votes for persons on the list of candidates. The votes from the electoral colleges in all the states were then sent to Washington and counted by the president of the Senate. The person found to have the greatest number of votes would then be president; the person with the next greatest number would be vice president.

On December 4, the electors cast their ballots. Weeks passed while the returns trickled in over the lonely roads and wilderness trails of the sixteen states. When the count was completed, victory was assured the Republicans, with seventy-three electoral votes for Jefferson against sixty-five for Adams, who had run well ahead of his party. But the Republicans had cast their second votes all too solidly for Burr, tying him for the top office with Jefferson.

Thus two candidates had an equal number of votes. What was to happen now? In this situation the Constitution provided that the election should be thrown into the House, that is, that the House of Representatives should choose. "If," said the Constitution,

*there be more than one who have . . . an equal number of votes, then the House of Representatives shall immediately choose by ballot one of them for President. . . . In every case, after the choice of President, the* person *having the greatest number of votes of the electors shall be Vice-President."*

The Republicans in the election had swept the House of Representatives, but the new Congress would not come into session until March, 1801. The choice between the two Republican candidates, therefore—irony of ironies!—fell to the lame-duck House dominated by the old Federalist majority.

From New York, Hamilton tried openly to swing Federalist votes to Jefferson. In Washington's time, he had been Jefferson's greatest opponent. But he feared Burr even more.

It was a close fight, with each state delegation allowed no more than one vote. The initial balloting gave eight states to Jefferson, six to Burr. Two more states were divided. The vote of a single state stood between Jefferson and the presidency. Then after thirty-five ballots and six days of deadlock, James Bayard, the single representative of Delaware, switched his vote from Burr to Jefferson amid the anguished outcries of his party colleagues. The Virginia Republican became president of the United States.

"As far as accounts have been received from the various parts of the Union," reported the New York *Gazette and General Advertiser,*

*the election of Mr. Jefferson to the presidency has produced the liveliest feelings of joy. In Baltimore, Philadelphia, and New York, the bells have been rung and artillery been fired and convivial entertainment been given. In various places preparations are [in the] making*

*The Senate wing of the Capitol Building,
Washington, D.C., by William Birch.*

*for celebrating this great event on a scale proportionate to its magnitude.*

At noon on March 4, 1801, the president-elect left his boardinghouse at the foot of Capitol Hill and walked up the slope to the new home of the U.S. Congress, a three-story oblong of sandstone that would in time become the north wing of the Capitol. Plainly dressed in a broadcloth coat and knee breeches, he made his way to the Senate Chamber to be sworn in as third president of the United States—the first chief executive to take the oath in the muddy new capital city.

In his inaugural address, Jefferson spoke quietly and never raised his voice. He addressed himself as much to the divided nation as to the crowded gallery that had to strain to hear him; his speech was a plea for harmony and unity among the people. "We are all Republicans," he said, "we are all Federalists. . . . Let us, fellow-citizens, unite with one heart and one mind. Let us restore to social intercourse that harmony and affection without which liberty and even life itself are but dreary things."

The tone of the address was welcomed by men of both parties. William Rand, editor of *The Washington Federalist* and one of Jefferson's severest critics during the campaign, found the speech "replete with wisdom and moderation," and added, "It is worthy of a President of the United States."

But the bitterness of partisan politics had left deep scars: ex-President Adams had boarded a northbound stage the very morning of Inauguration Day to avoid the bitterness of witnessing the triumph of the Republican enemy who had once been his friend. As the coach bore Adams homeward toward Boston, the chief justice of the United States, John Marshall, administered the oath of office to the new president. Marshall was a staunch Federalist who had been appointed to his office during the last few weeks of the Adams administration; between him and Jefferson there existed a fear and hatred of electrical intensity. As for Jefferson and Aaron Burr, their political cooperation during the electoral campaign had dissolved—they had become rival contestants for the presidency itself. Throughout the hectic balloting in the House during January, 1801, Burr kept a promise that he had made to Jefferson and refrained from pressing his own candidacy. But he did not withdraw from the race; the new president did not forget this. The time would come during his administration when he would have the power and the opportunity to revenge himself upon Burr.

Frustrated in Washington, Aaron Burr returned to New York and ran for governor of the state in 1804. For a second time, Hamilton blocked his candidacy. In March, 1804, the Albany *Register* reported, "Hamilton has come out decidedly against Burr . . . he spoke of him as a dangerous man and ought not to be trusted." Hamilton's position was made known just before the election. Burr was not elected.

For Burr this was the last straw. There was an angry exchange of letters and finally a challenge to a duel. In those days when a man felt that he had been insulted and his honor attacked, he was quick to demand satisfaction in terms of a fight with guns, knives, swords, or fists. In this case, then, Burr was the challenger.

The night before the duel, Burr wrote a farewell letter to his daughter Theodosia. Burr was a widower, and he had raised his girl himself; he had taught her Latin, Greek, French, literature, and history. She was married now to Joseph Alston, a South Carolina planter, but she remained her father's closest friend. "Having lately written my will," wrote Burr,

and given my private letters and papers in charge to you, I have no other direction to give you on the subject but to request you to burn all such as, if by accident made public, would injure any person. This is more particularly applicable to the letters of my female correspondents. All my letters and copies of letters, of which I have retained copies, are in the six blue boxes. If your husband or any one else (no one, however, could do it so well as he) should think it worth while to write a sketch of my life, some materials will be found among these letters. . . . I am indebted to you, my dearest Theodosia, for a very great portion of the happiness which I have enjoyed in this life. You have completely satisfied all that my heart and affections had hoped or even wished. With a little more perseverance, determination, and industry, you will obtain all that my ambition or vanity had fondly imagined. Let your son have occasion to be proud that he had a mother. Adieu. Adieu.

A. Burr.

Hamilton, too, settled his affairs and prepared for his executors a packet containing his will and a letter of explanation. He stressed the fact that dueling was hateful

*Corn column and capital from*
*the Capitol Building, Washington, D.C.*

to him, that he had no intention of harming Burr, but that he could not honorably avoid the encounter. "My religious and moral principles," he said,

are strongly opposed to the practice of duelling, and it would ever give me pain to be obliged to shed the blood of a fellow creature in a private combat forbidden by the laws. My wife and children are extremely dear to me, and my life is of the utmost importance to them, in various views. I feel a sense of obligation toward my creditors who in case of accident to me, by the forced sale of my property, may be in some degree sufferers. I did not think myself at liberty as a man of probity lightly to expose them to this hazard. I am conscious of no ill-will to Colonel Burr distinct from political opposition, which, I trust, has proceeded from pure and upright motives. . . . I shall hazard much, and can possibly gain nothing by the issue of the interview. But it was, as I conceive, impossible for me to avoid it. . . . My animadversions on the political principles, character and views of Colonel Burr have been extremely severe, and on different occasions, I, in common with many others, have made very unfavorable criticisms on particular instances of the private conduct of this gentleman.

Hamilton felt that if he backed down from this challege he would lose face with the public and his political career would be at an end. "The ability to be in future useful," he wrote, "whether in resisting mischief or effecting good, in those crises of our public affairs, which seem likely to happen, would probably be inseparable from a conformity with public prejudice in this particular." But though he felt obliged to go through with the duel, he stressed again that he had no intention of harming Burr. "If," he concluded,

our interview is conducted in the usual manner, and it pleases God to give me the opportunity, I have resolved to reserve and throw away my first fire, and I have thoughts even of reserving my second fire—and thus giving a double opportunity to Colonel Burr to pause and reflect.

Thus was inflicted upon Aaron Burr the humiliation of killing a man who had resolved not to defend himself. On July 12, 1804, news of Hamilton's death appeared in New York's *Evening Post*:

With emotions that we have not a hand to inscribe, have we to announce the death of ALEXANDER HAMIL-TON.

He was suddenly cut off in the forty-eighth year of his age, in the full vigor of his faculties and in the midst of all his usefulness.

We have not the firmness to depict this melancholy, heartrending event. Now—when death has extinguished all party animosity, the gloom that overspreads every countenance, the sympathy that pervades every bosom, bear irresistible testimony of the esteem and respect all maintained for him, of the love all bore him.

Hamilton left a wife and seven children. An eighth child, a son, had been killed three years before—in a duel at Weehawken.

In reporting the Burr-Hamilton encounter, both the

*Morning Chronicle* and the *New York Herald*, which reprinted the story, had concluded by saying:

*We conceive it proper to add that the conduct of both parties in this interview was perfectly proper as suited the occasion.*

Yet local feeling ran against Burr, and on August 4, the *New York Herald* announced:

*The Coroner's Inquest, after a very patient and laborious examination of the facts and circumstances relating to the late afflicting event, have pronounced upon their oaths that AARON BURR, Esq., Vice-President of the United States, was guilty of the MURDER of ALEXANDER HAMILTON.*

Burr fled New York and headed south until the storm blew over. Southerners were, at that time, more addicted to dueling than Northerners and less intolerant of those who fought and killed in this way. He found shelter and hospitality in the Georgia Sea Islands, at the palatial home of the rich Federalist and cotton planter, Pierce Butler.

# ☆| 3 |☆

## WHITE GOLD AND BLACK IRON

When Aaron Burr fled to Georgia, most of the state was still a wilderness of virgin forest. Fringing the coast were the Sea Islands, a long chain of semitropical islands standing between the Atlantic breakers and the mainland. Soon after the Revolution, these islands, by virtue of their good soil, ideal location, and climatic conditions, became a center of sugar, cotton, and rice production. Major Pierce Butler, Carolina planter and U.S. senator, was one of the first to bring slaves into this area and to profit from its fertility. The plantations which by 1800 were making him rich were located upon two islands at the mouth of the Altamaha River—Butler Island and St. Simons Island. "Major Butler's island in this river," wrote Burr to Theodosia, describing Butler Island near the town of Darien,

is one mile below the town. It must become fine rice country, for the water is fresh four miles below Major Butler's, and the tide rises from four to five feet, and the flats or swamps are from five to seven miles in width for a considerable distance up the river. . . . Honey of fine *flavor is found in great abundance in the woods about the mouth of the river, and, for aught I know, in every part of the country. You perceive that I am constantly discovering new luxuries for my table.*

The principal crop on St. Simons Island, where Burr passed most of his time, was cotton, known as white gold among the planters. The cotton mills of England took all of it that the Sea Islands could produce and begged for more. Julian Niemcewicz, a Polish visitor who traveled throughout the United States at this time, noted the widespread use of English fabrics made from American cotton. The English mills, he wrote, "use only cotton from Georgia and Carolina, which is of very good quality."

When Aaron Burr arrived in Georgia, a revolution in cotton production was under way, and in just a few short years, it was going to transform the face of the South.

The cotton that grew on the Sea Islands, and as early as 1790 was making a fortune for Major Butler and planters like him, was *Gossypium barbadense*, known as long-staple cotton. After the plant has flowered, its seeds mature in the seed pod, or boll; each seed is surrounded by a fluffy mass of silky fibers, each four or five inches in length. The cotton fibers could be separated easily enough from the seeds by hand or a simple machine. But the Sea Islands by themselves could not meet the ever-growing British demand for cotton; there simply wasn't enough land there for production.

Long-staple cotton flower (gossypium barbadense).

## John, John

"John, John" is one of the religious songs that the St. Simons Island slaves sang and that Aaron Burr would have heard if he had visited a prayer meeting. Lydia Parrish collected this version on St. Simons Island in the 1920s from Quarterman, whose mother was one of the Butler slaves.

MODERATELY FAST

John, John you will see John Aye John

John, John you will see John Aye John

Fi - ah in - a Eas' and Fi - ah in - a Wes'

Aye John Fi - ah gon - na burn out the

wil - der ness Aye John

SOLO an' fi-ah

*chorus*   John, John you will see John
                    Aye John
John, John you will see John
                    Aye John

Fiah in-a Eas' and fiah in-a Wes'
                    Aye John
Fiah gonna burn out the wilderness
                    Aye John
*chorus*

God in-a wilderness jes begin to look out
                    Aye John
Yes, the ram horn blow an'a children shout
                    Aye John
*chorus*

Talk about John and you will see John
                    Aye John
Talk about John but you will see John
                    Aye John
*chorus*

When I get to Heaven goin' to walk all aroun'
                    Aye John
Angel in-a Heaven can't order me down
                    Aye John
*chorus*

When I get to Heaven gonna sit and tell
                    Aye John
Gonna argue with the Father and chatter with the Son
                    Aye John
*chorus*


Well, couldn't cotton be grown on the mainland, in
the interior of Georgia and other Southern states? Yes
and no. No, in the sense that long-staple cotton could

only flourish in the moist, semitropical conditions of the coastal zone. Yes, in the sense that there *was* another variety of cotton adapted to the harsher conditions of the mainland. This cotton was *Gossypium hirsutum*, or short-staple cotton. But there was a problem with short-staple cotton. Its fibers were so firmly fixed to the seed that it was next to impossible to pull them off. Solve this technical problem of separating the fiber from the seed and *hirsutum* could inherit the South.

During the early 1790s, this problem became a favorite topic for dinner-table discussions in the South, and Catherine Greene's Mulberry Grove plantation near Savannah, Georgia, was no exception. Catherine was the widow of Nathanael Greene, the Revolutionary War general. Phineas Miller, the young manager of her estate, and his friend Eli Whitney were two Northerners who became closely interested in the discussions about cotton.

A Massachusetts farmer's son and recently graduated from Yale, Whitney had with Miller's help obtained a position as tutor to a South Carolina family. Although full of misgivings about the Georgia climate—he fully expected to die of malaria—the young man had come south in the vivacious Mrs. Greene's company and was only too delighted to break his journey at Mulberry Grove. He never got to South Carolina. In a letter written to his father in September, 1793, Whitney explained why.

*I went from New York with the family of the late Major General Greene. I went immediately with the family to their plantation about twelve miles from Savannah with expectations of spending four or five days and then pro-*

ceed into Carolina to take the school as I had mentioned in former letters.

During this time I heard much said of the extreme difficulty of ginning cotton, that is, separating it from its seed. There were a number of very respectable gentlemen at Mrs. Greene's who all agreed that if a machine could be invented which would clean the cotton with expedition, it would be a great thing both to the country and to the inventor.

Whitney was a mechanical genius. In his early teens during the Revolution, he had already demonstrated his skill by building all kinds of ingenious tools and setting up a workshop at his father's farm. Now he was fascinated by the challenge posed by his Southern hosts.

Whitney set to work, and in ten days he had produced an operating model of a cotton gin—a machine to gin cotton, or separate the seeds from the lint. How did the gin work? Perhaps the best short answer is to be found in the popular version of Whitney's discovery. Legend has it that he was sitting on a farm fence brooding about the problem. As he sat there, a cat stole up to the fence and put a paw through it to clutch a chicken on the other side. The bird's body slammed against the fence, and it ran squawking away. But the cat came away with some feathers. When he saw this, Eli yelled "Eureka!"—which is Greek for "ohmygosh, I've got it."

Of course, the story probably isn't true, but it explains the cotton gin pretty well. The cat-chicken-feather operation reflected the main principle of the machine. A series of hooks fitted onto a wooden drum tore into the cotton seeds as they were rotated through the slats of a wooden

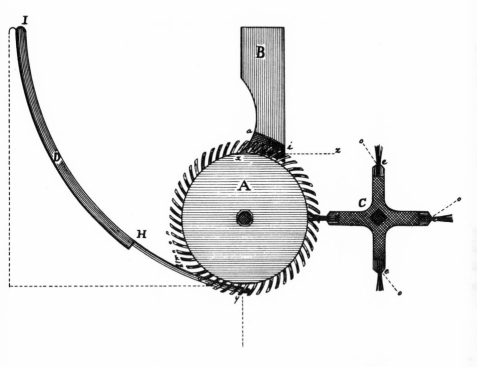

*Eli Whitney's cotton gin, diagram from U.S. Patent Office.*

"fence" dividing the box in which the drum was mounted. The drum could be turned by hand, by a horse, or by a steam engine. In this way hundreds of pounds of short-staple cotton could be ginned by one machine in the course of a single day.

As Whitney later reported to his father, he was immediately offered a hundred guineas for his machine, "if I would give up all right and title to it." It didn't take Whitney long to decide that his future was not in teaching.

*I concluded to relinquish my school and turn my attention to perfecting this machine. I made one before I came away which required the labor of one man to turn it and with which one man will clean ten times as much cotton as he can in any other way.*

To the amazement of those who watched the demonstration, a slave turning the hand crank was able to process the fiber at the rate of fifty pounds a day!

Not all those who came to examine Whitney's invention were "respectable gentlemen." While the inventor returned North in order to apply for a patent, the machine was widely copied. By 1800 the agricultural revolution was under way. Land values throughout the Deep South were rising. Planters in Virginia and the Carolinas were abandoning their worn-out acres and moving with their slaves to Georgia and Alabama to clear the virgin wilderness and seed it to cotton.

In 1792 the cotton crop had amounted to no more than 138,328 pounds. By 1794 that figure had risen to over a million and a half pounds, or nearly twelve times as much as the amount of two years before. By 1800 the South was producing 35 million pounds of cotton and selling it to eager mill owners in Old and New England.

In the eyes of cotton farmers and planters, the gin seemed to be indeed a great invention and a very fortunate thing. It also brought new life to the institution of slavery.

Cotton growing demanded great crews of workmen. It meant long hours of stooping under the burning sun tending the plants. At harvest time, it meant picking the white bolls and stuffing them into big shoulder sacks that grew progressively heavier as they were dragged between the rows. No free man wanted to do that kind of work. But an African, kidnapped from his home, transported to America, and sold on the auction block, had no choice.

Chances of escape were small. Julian Niemcewicz, traveling in the South in 1797, encountered a Maryland slaveholder bringing a runaway slave back from Pennsylvania.

*We stopped before the prison. A Negro, in breeches, vest, a torn shirt, and his hands tied with a handkerchief came out. One of our company, whom I discovered later to be his master, placed him among us.*

The company dined at Wilmington, on the Delaware side of the border. On leaving, the Polish traveler noticed that

*the poor Negro had manacles of iron on his hands. His master confided in me that he had fled two years before, that he was caught on the quayside in Philadelphia and he was taking him back home.*

The next day the stage passed by Havre de Grace, a new town thirty-seven miles from Baltimore.

*Two miles from there my fine gentleman got off with his negro. . . . Wretched humanity! He had his farm a half an hour away from there. God knows the fate that awaits the poor negro.*

After 1790 slavery in the North began to lose its hold; it was needed less and less in a land of small farms, craftsmen's shops, and commercial centers. But as slaves were freed in the North and their numbers diminished there, exactly the opposite happened in the South. More and more the institution came to be regarded as a necessity, and the numbers of black slaves began to climb.

In 1790 the total slave population for the entire United States came to no more than 648,000. By the turn of the century, however, the importation of 200,000 additional blacks had brought the slave population close to the million mark—nearly one-fifth of the total population of the United States. By 1810 the number of slaves soared to 1,154,282 and was still climbing. A healthy field hand brought from $300 to $500 at auction. Women of breeding age were equally valuable.

The slave trade, defined as the transportation of black slaves to America from Africa in United States or European ships, was outlawed by the Constitution in 1808; but in actual fact, it flourished illegally almost until the outbreak of the Civil War. A slave ship could carry four hundred to five hundred people in the hold. Fifteen or twenty percent may have died during the passage from Africa; enough usually survived to turn a nice profit for the shipowner from the voyage.

As early as 1790, agitation against the trade by the English Quakers, pioneer abolitionists, was turning up a mass of information which was placed before the British Parliament. One doctor who had served aboard a British slaver testified:

*The slaves are so crowded below that it is impossible to walk among them without treading upon them. I was never among them for ten minutes together below but my shirt was wet as if dipped in water. Many are lost to suffocation in the foul air of the hold. They are closely wedged together and have not so much room as a man in his coffin, either in length or breadth. Sometimes the dead and living are found shackled together. They go down appearing to be well at night and are found dead in the morning.*

Many who fell ill refused treatment, preferring death to slavery. Repeated instances were cited of slaves trying to leap overboard at sea. To prevent this, the decks were covered with heavy netting. "Notwithstanding," said one crewman, "they often attempt it, and sometimes succeed, showing signs of joy in the very jaws of death."

Putting aside the agonies of the slaves and their ruined lives, it seemed in the 1790s that planters of short-staple cotton could look forward to a rosy future. Whitney, along with the rest, dreamed of high profits from the sale of his gin. Leaving Phineas Miller as his Southern partner, he returned North, not only to get a patent for his invention from the federal government, but to set up a factory for the production of gins.

But the gin was too useful and too easy to copy to remain the property of two men alone. Whitney spent many years fighting patent infringements, loopholes in the patent law, and organized hostility among the plant-

*Black people in front of a Philadelphia bank. Painting by Pavel Petrovich Svinin.*

ers. They had grown rich, thanks to the gin, but they resented enriching its Yankee inventor—particularly if he charged fancy prices for ginning their cotton. Thus the South adopted Whitney's gin without asking his permission. His venture failed, and he cast around for another use for his talents.

The North that Eli had returned to was still mainly rural. Niemcewicz, traveling through Connecticut at this time, painted an idyllic picture of New England farming.

*The countryside alternates between valleys and hills; there are many meadows, some drained by ditches. Herds of domestic animals are seen more frequently than in other states, especially sheep. The fields, for the most part, are covered with maïs, rye, very little wheat, and are mostly bounded with stone walls.*

At the same time, industry was beginning to take root, and so were some of its evils. In Paterson, New Jersey, in 1805, an early cotton factory was already employing child labor.

*We went to see the cotton factory. It is enormous and fitted out to perfection. There are four floors filled with spinning machines and looms, all the machines driven by water. One can never see this astounding mechanism, by means of which a child can do more work than could two hundred hands, without paying tribute to the genius of the man who invented it. Three-quarters of these machines still remain idle because of the lack of hands. They employ only children from the age of 7 to 14.*

In southern New Jersey, iron was being mined and then smelted in the nation's first large foundries. Wherever water power could be found to turn wheels, new industries were springing up. It didn't take Whitney long to realize that his future lay in the industrial North rather than the agrarian South. In 1798 he wrote to Oliver Wolcott, the secretary of the treasury, offering to provide the government with muskets. Once again, his timing was perfect. Relations between the French Republic and the Adams administration had reached an all-time low, and war with France seemed imminent. The government was in serious need of arms. Whitney now proposed to provide ten thousand muskets or more—at least one-third of the total amount required by the army.

It was an unbelievable offer to make in an age when every machine part, down to the smallest screw, was laboriously turned out by hand. Even a row of skilled gunsmiths, working in a traditional craftsman's shop, would labor forever at such an assignment. But that was not what Whitney had in mind. For one thing, America lacked skilled craftsmen; the shortage had kept her dependent on British manufacturing.

". . . very few really good experienced workmen in this branch of business are to be had in this country," Whitney wrote to Wolcott.

*In order to supply ourselves in the course of the next few years with any considerable number of really good muskets, such means must be devised as will preclude the necessity of every workman's being bred to the business.*

Whitney was talking about muskets, but his experience at turning out cotton gins had led him to realize that the making of almost any product could be reduced to a number of stages, each of which could be easily learned by an unskilled laborer. But first he proposed to create machine tools that would turn out standardized and interchangeable parts.

*One of my primary objects is to form the tools so the tools themselves shall fashion the work and give to every part its just proportion—which when once accomplished, will give expedition, uniformity, and exactness to the whole.*

"In short," Whitney concluded, "the tools which I contemplate are similar to an engraving on copper plate from which may be taken a great number of impressions perceptibly alike."

As in the South, Whitney saw a need and filled it. Down in Georgia the problem had been that of separating the cotton from the seeds. In the North it was a matter of creating and assembling the parts of an intricate machine in a series of automatic steps, by-passing the need for the specialized master mechanic. The days of the craftsman were already numbered.

The Federalists had been promoters of industry, and Whitney's first slow steps in setting up his system were met favorably by the Adams administration. Ironically, it was Thomas Jefferson who as president provided further encouragement and, more importantly, financial assistance. Back in 1793 Jefferson, then secretary of state, had first received Whitney's application for a cotton gin patent. As a Southern planter and as an inventor of ingenuity, he knew how to appreciate the New Englander's achievement.

Nevertheless, Whitney was worried as he left for Washington in December, 1800, a demonstration musket under

*A tobacco plantation.*

his arm. Politics meant little to him, but how much would they mean to the man who would certainly be president in two months? Would Whitney's Federalist ties be held against him? The interview followed in January, 1801.

"We last evening waited upon Mr. Jefferson, in pursuance of a previous appointment. He had while in France & England, by direction of this Government particularly attended to the Manufacture of Arms."

Thus wrote Elizur Goodrich, congressman from Connecticut and close friend to Whitney. The demonstration model was brought out for inspection. Jefferson was fascinated.

"On a very critical survey & examination," continued Goodrich, *he did not hesitate to say, that he had in no instance seen any work or specimens equal to Mr. Whitney's, excepting in one factory in France in which the owner had defined the various parts of his Muskets, on the principles of Mr. Whitney . . . that by Authority of this Country at great price he attempted to remove this Artist to the United States—but he was immediately taken into the service of the Crown, and had since deceased. He observed that the manufacture of Arms, even at double expense, must be secured, that Arms however of equal goodness could not be so cheaply produced from any part of Europe.*

Jefferson immediately proposed that Whitney furnish arms to the state of Virginia, in addition to those contracted for by the federal government. Several times after that, the two men got together to talk shop. The small arms manufacturer from New England had found a powerful ally in the agrarian-minded, peace-loving president from Virginia.

Whitney had set up his factory at Mill Rock, Connecticut, outside New Haven in 1798. With its workshops, storehouses, workers' living quarters, and waterfall to power the machinery, it was a little mill town and one of the first of its kind.

At the iron foundry in Mount Hope, New Jersey, Niemcewicz observed another early industrial community.

*Here and there are scattered the houses of the workers; on the left hand is a large lake which provides the water for the mills. The horizon on all sides is lined with mountains covered with forests. Four shafts provide the main access to the iron ore, which is the raw material. The deepest are 30 to 40 feet; two or three people work in each one. From one hundred to two hundred souls, counting women and children, belong to this tremendous undertaking. . . . The owner keeps a store, from which he provides food, drink, and clothing, etc., taking the money from their pay and reserving 10 per cent for himself.*

The cotton gin was changing the face of the South. In time, the mill town would change the face of the North, attracting farmers off the land and later absorbing the unskilled masses pouring in from Europe.

But if there was to be manufacturing, there had to be a market. And that market lay beyond the Alleghenies, among the settlers of the Ohio, Cumberland, and Tennessee valleys. For the North as well as the South, the settlement of the western territories would be a crucial factor in the development of their economic life.

☆| 4 |☆

# A MONUMENTAL BARGAIN

In 1802 New Orleans was a lively, bustling city. Situated at the mouth of the Mississippi, the gulf port was hostess to people of all kinds—planters from the United States and the West Indies, French colonists, or Creoles, Spanish traders, backwoods settlers, and rivermen.

Beyond the city lay the flat, rich bottom lands of the Mississippi Delta, where cypress swamps gave way to lush plantations. Farther inland and to the east lay the great southern wilderness—the ancient homeland of the Alabama, Natchez, Creek, Choctaw, Chickasaw, Cherokee, and other Indian tribes.

In 1818 Estwick Evans, a New Hampshire lawyer seeing the town for the first time, wrote that it appeared "large, ancient, and populous."

*I entered the city at noon day. Its streets were crowded with people of every description. Perhaps no place in the world, excepting Vienna, contains a greater variety of the human race than New Orleans. Besides foreigners of all nations, there are here a various population peculiarly its own. These are of every shade of complexion.*

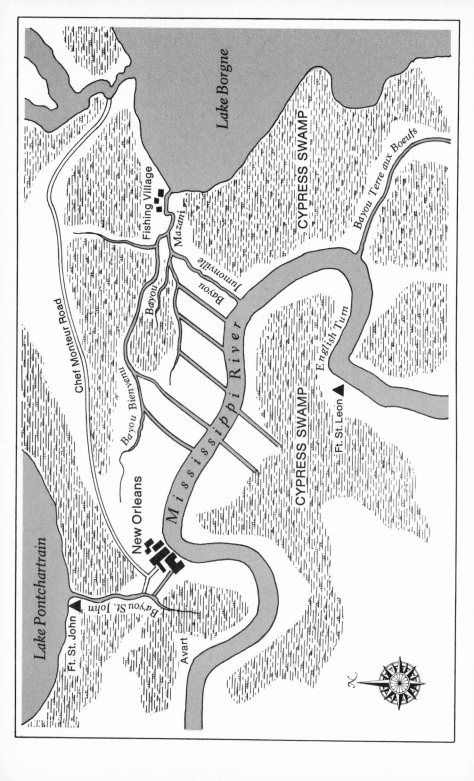

Evans noted that the land in the Mississippi Delta was "low and level," with the city standing "immediately upon the bank, and upon a curve or bend in the river."

*The water is kept from flowing into the city by a Levee or embankment, which was raised by the Spanish government. The Levee extends from Fort Plaquemine, about forty miles below the city, to one hundred and twenty miles above it. This embankment is about four feet high and fifteen feet wide. A great deal has been said respecting this road; but it is not deserving of much notice. The undertaking was not great, and its execution displays no ingenuity or neatness. All the market-people bring their produce upon the Levee; and here the inhabitants of the place take their evening walk.*

The overrated levee notwithstanding, Evans was impressed with the size and layout of the town.

*The city extends, on the river, about a mile and a quarter. The streets cross each other at right angles, and the side walks of some of them are paved with flat stones or bricks. . . . At the upper part of the city, near the river, is the Custom-House; and at the lower part of it is the Fort and Cantonment. Not far from these is a spacious establishment, which is occupied by an association of Nuns. The Cathedral stands near the centre of the town.*

The port's bustling commercial life earned the Yankee's wholehearted admiration.

*Vast quantities of provisions of every kind, proceed from the Ohio, the Mississippi, and their tributaries, for the consumption of the people of New Orleans, for ship stores, and for foreign markets. . . .*

*The city of New Orleans is a place of immense business. In the course of fifty years it will probably be, in a mercantile point of view, second to none in the world. At this place inland and maritime commerce combine their energies.*

In 1800 Isaac Weld had seen western farmers pole their crops downstream to the New Orleans markets. Although the port was the property of Spain at that time, United States people were free to ship their goods to New Orleans and sell them there. This privilege, or "right of deposit," had been won from the Spanish government by the Adams administration in 1795. The agreement gave United States people the right to deposit goods in the port and to use its facilities freely for their trade.

Thus when Jefferson became president, New Orleans was the American West's gateway to the sea. But what if New Orleans changed hands or came under the control of a government hostile to the United States? If the port were closed, it would become a noose, strangling the economic life of the hinterland. This is precisely the danger that threatened. On November 26, 1802, Samuel Harrison Smith's *National Intelligencer* announced to its Washington readers:

*We are informed that the Executive has received advice, that the port of NEW ORLEANS has been closed against foreign vessels from the ocean, including American, and that the right of depositing American property there has been prohibited without any other establishment being assigned in lieu of it. These regulations, so contrary to our treaty with Spain, were published at New Orleans by the intendant on the 17th October last.*

Newspapers in that day did not go in for scare head-lines. The news was tucked away in a column of local notes, halfway down an inside page. But its importance did not escape Washington. Senate and House members from Kentucky and Tennessee were appalled that their people at home should be prohibited an outlet for their products. As the news filtered inland from Washington and up from the gulf, angry protests arrived from the settlements. The frontiersmen threatened to organize expeditions of their own to march on New Orleans if the government did not take effective action.

Notwithstanding the continuation of Spanish govern-ment in New Orleans, Jefferson knew perfectly well, in 1802, that Louisiana was no longer under Spanish control. Louisiana was the name that the French had given, in the seventeenth century, to their American empire—that vast stretch of land that lay between the Rocky Mountains and the Appalachians, the Canadian forests and the Gulf of Mexico. All of this had been French until it was taken from them by war in 1763; the eastern half was turned over to the British, and the western half to the Spanish. Now, in 1800, Napoleon dreamed of taking it all back again, of building a mighty French empire in the heart of North America.

Thus in that year, Louisiana changed hands as a result of a secret treaty between Napoleon and his royal puppet, the weakling Charles IV of Spain. All of the land between the Mississippi and the Rockies, together with the port of New Orleans, became the property of France. And then in October, 1802, the blow fell. The American right of deposit was simply prohibited without any reason being given.

Months before the port of New Orleans was closed to American shipping, Jefferson had taken action. In April of 1802 he had entrusted an old friend of his, the distinguished economist Pierre DuPont de Nemours, with a letter addressed to the American minister in Paris, Robert Livingston. The letter was unsealed, and DuPont was an advisor to the French government. The letter was addressed to Livingston, but its contents were aimed at Napoleon.

"The cession of Louisiana and the Floridas by Spain to France," wrote Jefferson, "works most sorely on the United States."

*It completely reverses all the political relations of the United States, and will form a new epoch in our political course. Of all nations of any consideration, France is the one which, hitherto, has offered the fewest points on which we could have any conflict of rights, and most points of a communion of interests.*

*From these causes, we have ever looked to her as our natural friend, as one with which we never could have an occasion of differences.*

But as Jefferson was quick to point out, every friendship has its limits.

*There is on the globe one single spot, the possessor of which is our natural and habitual enemy. It is New Orleans, through which the product of three-eighths of our territory must pass to market, and from its fertility it will ere long yield more than half of our whole product, and contain more than half of our inhabitants. France placing herself in that door, assumes to us the attitude of defiance.*

After noting that two dynamic nations such as France and the U.S. would make uncongenial neighbors, Jefferson concluded with a threat and an offer.

*The day that France takes possession of New Orleans, fixes the sentence which is to restrain her forever within her low-water mark. It seals the union of two nations, who, in conjunction, can maintain exclusive possession of the ocean. From that moment, we must marry ourselves to the British fleet and nation. . . . If France considers Louisiana, however, as indispensable for her views, she might perhaps be willing to look about for arrangements which might reconcile it to our interests. If anything could do this, it would be the ceding to us the island of New Orleans and the Floridas. This would certainly, in a great degree, remove the causes of jarring and irritation between us.*

Throughout 1802 Jefferson quietly waited for some word on his purchase offer and/or a new European war to distract the French dictator. In Paris Livingston hammered away at the American proposal without success. It was a discouraging job. At times it seemed as if his only satisfaction lay in his association with a fellow expatriate, Robert Fulton, a painter-turned-engineer who was fascinated with the idea of propelling ships by steam. Fulton's first model, driven by a great steam-powered paddle wheel, had already enjoyed a trial run on the River Seine, and all Paris was talking about it. But Livingston's own mission, it seemed, had foundered. Talleyrand, Napoleon's inscrutable foreign minister, refused to commit himself.

Suddenly in December, 1802, there was a new tone in Livingston's correspondence.

"Pray be explicit in the amount of what I may offer," he wrote. "The peace with England will not be lasting."

In response, Secretary of State Madison sent Livingston an assistant—James Monroe—with instructions to "procure a cession of New Orleans and the Floridas to the United States and consequently of the Mississippi as the boundary between the United States and Louisiana." Livingston was annoyed. With a record of public service dating back to the Continental Congress, he resented the implication that he needed the help of one of Jefferson's Virginia friends.

But Livingston soon forgot his hurt feelings. Monroe had hardly arrived in Paris, in the spring of 1803, when Talleyrand called Livingston in and asked, did the Americans wish to buy the whole of Louisiana?

Livingston was dumfounded by the offer. He had asked just for the city of New Orleans—and he had been offered an empire! Livingston dashed off an excited letter to Madison to report the conversation. "I told him [Talleyrand] no," he wrote,

*that our wish extended only to New Orleans and the Floridas; that the policy of France, however, should dictate . . . to give us the country above the River Arkansas, in order to place a barrier between them and Canada. He said that if they gave New Orleans the rest would be of little value, and that he would wish to know "what we would give for the whole."*

What had brought about this extraordinary change in French policy?

Early in 1803 Napoleon, with typical impetuosity, decided that he would get rid of Louisiana and sell it to the Americans. The fact is that his ambitions to rebuild an American empire had suffered a major blow with the disaster that had overtaken his military forces in Santo Domingo.

To move into the New World, Napoleon needed a base of operations in the Caribbean. Thus his first objective was to recapture control of the French colony of Santo Domingo. From here his ships would have clear sailing into the Gulf of Mexico and up the Mississippi.

Santo Domingo was a French sugar colony where tens of thousands of black slaves toiled under the lash of their white masters. When the French Revolution came in 1789, the Blacks took matters into their own hands, rose in revolt, and plunged the Caribbean island into an era of bloody war. The leader of the Black state which the ex-slaves set up was Toussaint L'Ouverture, general-in-chief of Santo Domingo, military genius, and Spartacus of the New World.

By 1801 Napoleon was ready to settle accounts with these upstart Blacks. French armies invaded the island and captured Toussaint. He was sent back to France in irons, and he died of starvation and neglect in a French dungeon.

But the island war went on without Toussaint; by the spring of 1803, the French expeditionary forces had suffered a crushing defeat. They were mired down in unending guerrilla warfare with half a million Blacks who would die, but would not return to slavery. Two French armies had vanished—almost thirty thousand men had died either in combat or from the dreaded yellow fever. Millions of francs had been spent, but there seemed no end to the demand for men and money. The French commander, General Leclerc, was still sending in frantic

*Toussaint L'Ouverture, hero of the Black revolution of Santo Domingo.*

requests for more of both. And then, he, too, died of yellow fever.

Thus Napoleon made his swift decision. He would resume his interrupted war with England, and he would become master of Europe. Later, when he controlled the riches of the Old World, he would settle accounts with the New. In the meantime, let the Americans have Louisiana: he would cast it to them like a bone. It might—who knows?—bring them into collision with his British enemy!

When Lucien and Joseph Bonaparte, Napoleon's brothers, heard that Louisiana was to be sold to the Americans, they were furious. The ambitious Lucien had counted upon being made governor of Louisiana; Joseph was angry that his brother would do such a thing without even asking his advice, that he would "sell Louisiana with as little ceremony as our dear father would have shown in selling a vineyard."

So they called upon Napoleon when he was taking a bath. While they ranted and raved at him, the first consul sat in the tub and listened "in excellent humor." The valet, who was a new man on the job, patiently held a towel and listened to the tirade along with his master.

What happened then was recorded by Lucien in his memoirs.

*The matter seemed about to be dropped, and Joseph and I were turning toward the door when Napoleon cried from the tub: "Well, sirs, think what you please about the sale of Louisiana. But you may both of you put on mourning. You, Lucien, over the sale of your province. You, Joseph, because I propose to dispense with the consent of all persons whoever. Do you hear?"*

Joseph, stung by his words and manner, especially by the contemptuous "Do you hear?" rushed back, exclaiming: "You will do well, my dear brother, not to lay your plans before the Chamber, for I swear to you I will put myself, if necessary, at the head of the opposition which will certainly be made!"

This brought an outburst from Napoleon of loud and sarcastic laughter. Joseph flushed, and stuck his face right into Napoleon's as he sat there, up to his neck in bathwater. "Laugh," he screamed, "laugh, laugh, then! Nevertheless, I shall do as I say. Although I do not like to mount the tribune, this time you will see me there!"

"You insolent fellow! I ought—!" Napoleon rose up in the tub and abruptly fell back. Joseph received full in the face the splash from the tub, which also drenched his clothes.

Now the valet fell to the floor in a fainting fit. Our Corsican tempers instantly cooled. Joseph picked him up. I rang the servants' bell. And Napoleon, his face just visible over the bathtub's edge, said, sympathetically, "Carry off the poor fellow and take good care of him."

Thus it was that French minister Talleyrand, over the violent objections of Joseph and Lucien, made to Livingston and Monroe the offer to sell Louisiana. The date was April 12, 1803. Spring had come to Paris. The chestnut and plane trees were in new leaf and the patterned gardens of the Tuileries were gay with Holland tulips. It was a year since Jefferson had penned his first instructions to Livingston, and the American minister was in a wonderful mood.

Livingston first of all offered 20 million francs for Louisiana, a sum that Talleyrand thought "a little low." Days of haggling followed, each offer and counteroffer dutifully reported by Livingston. Monroe, because of his late arrival, remained discreetly in the background. The two American ministers were acting completely on their own, assuming a responsibility for which they had no precedent in international diplomacy. But the slowness of communication—two months or more for an exchange of letters across the Atlantic—left them no choice. They remembered a remark made by a friendly minister early in the bargaining: "You know the temper of the youthful dictator. Everything he does is rapid as lightning."

On April 30, Livingston sent off the following dispatch:

*We have the honor to inform you that a treaty has been signed between the Minister Plenipotentiary of the French Government and ourselves by which the United States have obtained the full right and sovereignty in and over New Orleans and the whole of Louisiana.*

The price agreed upon amounted to $15,000,000 in gold.

Though elated, President Jefferson was beset with misgivings. The purchase would, of course, more than double the territory of the United States. The Republicans, however, had always stood for a strict interpretation of the Constitution, and there was nothing in the Constitution providing specifically for the purchase of foreign territory. Would a constitutional amendment—a long and time-consuming process—be necessary and an opportunity be lost in the meantime? Someone among his advisers found

*Political cartoon by James Gillray, 1805, showing Napoleon and Pitt "devouring" the western world.*

the solution in Section 2 of Article III, which states that the president

*shall have Power, by and with the Advice and Consent of the Senate, to make Treaties, provided two-thirds of the Senators present concur. . . .*

Despite violent opposition from the New England Federalists, who feared being politically swamped by an expanded west, the Senate approved the purchase on October 17, 1803. Jefferson had made the greatest real estate bargain in American history.

Americans were aware that they were buying half a continent. Three months before Senate ratification of the purchase, Jefferson's young secretary, Meriwether Lewis, had written to his friend and former commander, William Clark:

*Very sanguine expectations are at this time formed by our government that the whole of that immense country watered by the Mississippi and its tributary streams, Missouri inclusive, will be the property of the United States in less than twelve months from this date.*

The Louisiana Purchase agreement had drawn no precise boundary lines; it specified only the lands drained by the Mississippi and its western tributaries. The question of those boundaries would remain unanswered for years to come. Yet the prize was rich enough. A great inland river system was now the property of the United States. Where did those rivers lead to? What kind of lands did they drain? And would one of them lead to the Pacific Ocean? In a little over half a year, Meriwether Lewis and his friend Billy Clark would be leading an expedition up the Missouri to find out.

## Lowlands

With New Orleans in French hands the marketing of much southern cotton would have been impossible. Shanties or work songs like this were sung by sailors loading cotton onto ships bound for New York and Liverpool.

INTRODUCTION

Low - lands, Low - lands, - way my John, Low -

lands a - way, I heard them say My

SOLO

dol - lar and a half a day. A

dol - lar and a half a day is a

CHORUS

nig - ger's pay, Low - lands,

SOLO

Low - lands a - way my John, I

CHORUS

thought I heard our Old Man say, My

dol - lar and a half a day!

low - lands

introduction   Lowlands, Lowlands, away my John,
        Lowlands away, I heard them say
        My dollar and a half a day.

1. A dollar and a half a day is a nigger's pay
   *chorus*   Lowlands, Lowlands, away my John,
   I thought I heard our Old Man say,
   *chorus*   My dollar and a half a day.

2. A white man's pay is rather high.
   *chorus*   Lowlands, Lowlands, away my John.
   A black man's pay is rather low,
   *chorus*   My dollar and a half a day.

3. I packed me bag and I'm bound away
   *chorus*   Lowlands, Lowlands, away my John.
   I'm bound away for Mobile Bay,
   *chorus*   My dollar and a half a day.

4. We're bound away for Mobile Bay,
   *chorus*   Lowlands, Lowlands, away my John,
   We're bound away at the break of day
   *chorus*   My dollar and a half a day.

5. Oh say, wuz ye never down in Mobile Bay?
   *chorus*   Lowlands, Lowlands, away my John.
   A-screwin' cotton all the day,
   *chorus*   My dollar and a half a day.

6. We'll heave 'er up from down below
   *chorus*   Lowlands, Lowlands, away my John.
   Oh, heave her up an' away we'll go!
   *chorus*   My dollar and a half a day.

7. Oh, I thought I heard the Old Man say,
   *chorus*   Lowlands, Lowlands, away my John,
   He'd give us rum three times a day,
   *chorus*   My dollar and a half a day.

# ACROSS THE WIDE MISSOURI:
# LEWIS AND CLARK

The date was May 14, 1804. Under a wet sky dull as old pewter, the brown Missouri River swept into the Mississippi between banks of new-green cottonwoods and willows. A long keelboat and two pirogues—canoes hollowed out of tree trunks—rode the rolling current, heading upstream. The Lewis and Clark expedition was on its way into the unexplored West.

There were forty-eight men, all in all, gathered into an army unit and under army discipline. The pay for privates was $5 a month, for sergeants, $8. They were a tough group of young soldiers and frontiersmen, recruited from the stockades of the Ohio Valley and the backwoods of Kentucky.

*Rained the fore part of the day. A heavy rain this afternoon. I set out at 4 o'clock P.M. in the presence of many of the neighboring inhabitants, and proceeded on under a gentle breeze up the Missouri. . . .*

The entry was made by William Clark, the tall, redheaded army officer whom Meriwether Lewis had chosen as his coleader. Lewis himself was still downriver at the little French settlement of St. Louis, but he would be traveling overland to join the party in two days.

More than a year's work, first by Lewis, then by Lewis and Clark together, had gone into the preparation for this day. But the idea of the expedition was far older than that. Exploring the Far West had been on Jefferson's mind since the early 1790s. At a time when the frontier began at the Alleghenies, the wild country on the other side of the Mississippi must have seemed as remote to most Americans as the far side of the moon. The Ohio, though plunging deep into Indian territory, was at least a known quantity. But little if anything was known about the great Missouri River which came tumbling down from the west, its waters brown with the soil of the northern plains.

As far as some explorers and fur trappers knew, a great snowcapped mountain range stood between those plains and the western shore, where American ships traded for furs with the coastal Indians. But what manner of country lay in between? From somewhere within that country, another great river, the Columbia, flowed to the Pacific. Did the Missouri lead to that western river? Was it, in other words, the answer to the age-old quest for a water passage across the continent? And what were American chances of cashing in on the rich fur trade that thrived along its banks?

Until the Louisiana Territory was officially transferred to the United States, President Jefferson had ordered the objective of the expedition kept secret. To equip it, he had obtained an appropriation of $2,500 from Congress, with the vague explanation that it was "for the purpose of extending the external commerce of the United States."

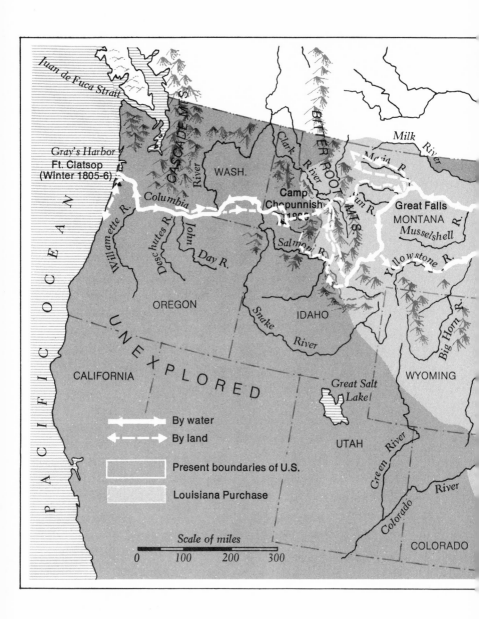

Juan de Fuca Strait

Gray's Harbor
Ft. Clatsop
(Winter 1805-6)

PACIFIC OCEAN

CASCADE MTS.

Columbia

Willamette R.

Deschutes R.

John

Day R.

WASH.

Columbia R.

Clark River

BITTER ROOT MTS.

Camp
Chopunnish
1806

Salmon River

Sun R.

Milk River

Maria R.

Great Falls

MONTANA

Musselshell R.

Yellowstone R.

OREGON

Snake River

IDAHO

Big Horn R.

U N E X P L O R E D

CALIFORNIA

Great Salt
Lake

WYOMING

UTAH

Green River

Colorado

River

By water

By land

Present boundaries of U.S.

Louisiana Purchase

COLORADO

Scale of miles
0      100     200     300

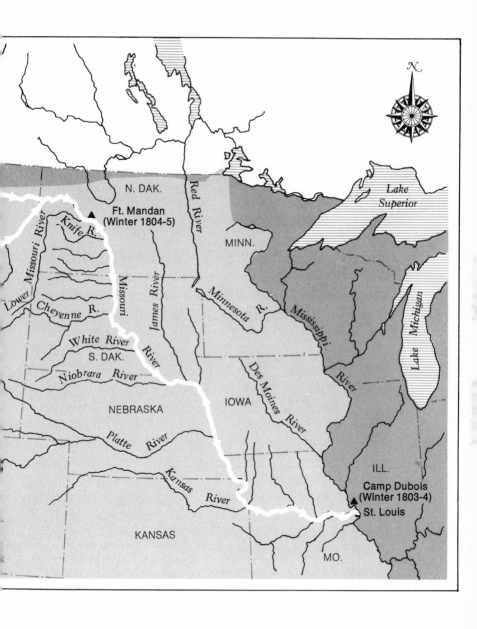

In April, 1803, Lewis received the president's instructions.

*The object of your mission is to explore the Missouri river, and such principal streams of it, as, by its course and communication with the waters of the Pacific Ocean, whether the Columbia, Oregon, Colorado, or any other river, may offer the most direct and practicable water-communication across the continent, for the purposes of commerce.*

The United States had won, in Louisiana, an empire of land whose extent was at that time unknown. Its vastness and its beauty was something to make men marvel. John Bradbury, an English botanist who traveled through it at this time, has left us his impression of the prairies and rolling grasslands that stretched westward to the Rockies.

*The territory west of the Mississippi belonging to the United States and extending from that river to the Rocky Mountains has evidently two characters, so distinct, as regards the external appearance, that they cannot justly be included in one general description. The part which lies immediately on the Mississippi, and extends from one hundred to two hundred and fifty miles westward from that river, has a thin covering of timber, consisting of clumps and of scattered trees. From the western limits of this region to the Rocky Mountains, the whole is one vast prairie or meadow, and, excepting on the alluviation of the rivers, and in a few instances, on the sides of the small hills, is entirely divested of trees or shrubs. The extent of this region is not accurately known, on account of the real*

situation of the Rocky Mountains not yet being truly
ascertained. . . .

Lewis and Clark and their company, setting out from
St. Louis, were to find out, among other things, the "real
situation" of the Rocky Mountains.

Enough was known of the lower Missouri to enable
the expedition to form some kind of preliminary plan.
They would first follow the Missouri upriver through
what would later be the states of Missouri, Nebraska,
Iowa, and North and South Dakota. On the uncharted
part of their journey the following spring, they would be
following the westward bend of the great river through
Montana to its source in the Rockies, passing across the
Continental Divide in Idaho, and following the westward-
flowing rivers down into the future states of Washington
and Oregon.

It was also to be a map-making expedition, charting
unexplored territory. The party was to make note of the
soil, vegetation, animals, "the mineral productions of
every kind," climate, and even "the dates at which particular plants put forth or lose their flower or leaf, times of
appearance of particular birds, reptiles or insects."

President Jefferson instructed the explorers to deal with
the Indians

in the most friendly and conciliatory manner which their
own conduct will admit; allay all jealousies as to the object
of your journey; satisfy them of its innocence; make them
acquainted with the position, extent, character, peaceable
and commercial dispositions of the United States; of our

*Meriwether Lewis and William Clark
holding council with the Indians.*

*wish to be neighborly, friendly, and useful to them, and of our dispositions to a commercial intercourse with them. . . .*

The explorers were even advised to take along the newly developed smallpox vaccine, with the idea of introducing its use among the Indians. At the same time, they were to find out everything they could about these peoples who still controlled the western rivers and the western fur trade.

The boats pushed to the northwest, across what would later become Missouri, and over to Iowa and Nebraska. The Corps of Discovery, as it was called, was aiming for the country of the Mandan Indians, a friendly people living in the territory later known as North Dakota. There they hoped to camp for the winter.

By mid-August they had passed the Platte River below the site of the present city of Omaha, having covered some six hundred miles in sixty-nine days. Each boat was rigged with a square sail, but on most days, it was the men bending over the oars that drove them westward. They were now in a land of primeval prairie, sodded deep in grasses as old as time.

"Lewis and I went up the bank and walked a short distance in the high prairie," Clark recorded in his log.

*This prairie is covered with grass 10 and 12 inches in height, soil of good quality. At the distance of about a mile still further back the country rises about 80 or 90 feet higher, and is one continued plain as far as can be seen. From the bluff on the second rise immediately above our camp, the most beautiful prospect of the river up and down and the country opposite presented itself which I ever beheld; the river meandering the open and beautiful plains, interspersed with groves of timber, such as willow, cotton, some mulberry, elm, sycamore, lynn [linden] and ash.*

Both men enjoyed their strolls away from the river-bank, but Lewis especially appreciated the solitude of the wilderness. He was the more introspective of the two, suffering spells of moodiness when the only company he wanted was the forest or prairie. Clark, by contrast, was cheerful and even-tempered. The two young men were good friends, the sons of neighboring families from Mr. Jefferson's own Albemarle County in Virginia. No two men could have been better suited to share the hardships and adventures before them. Both were six feet tall, lean and rugged, intelligent, and trained to make quick decisions from years of experience in the frontier army. In addition, they were well educated for their time, with a fair understanding of botany and geology, map making, and the use of the sextant and compass. Both were superb woodsmen.

Proud and independent Indian tribes—Sioux, Minnetaree, Arikara, Mandan, and many more—inhabited the northern plains. The Corps carried gifts for them, medals, beads, and jackets. As the journey proceeded, these gifts were distributed amid ceremonious talk and Lewis would tell the chiefs,

*Your old fathers, the French and Spaniards, have gone beyond the great lake toward the rising sun, and you are now the children of the great chief of the seventeen great nations of America.*

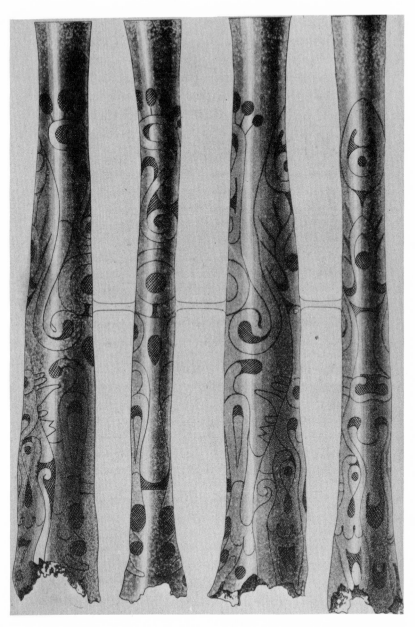

*Elk bones sculpted by Indians, found in Indian graves in Ohio.*

The Indians would then be assured that the great new chief controlled the rivers and that his traders would see to their wants. Lewis would issue a formal invitation—complete with a signed document—asking the chiefs to visit Washington as guests of the great American chief, President Jefferson. Tough little Sergeant Gass, who left his own record of the expedition, later sighed that the speech became "monotonously familiar as the expedition councided with one tribe after another during the next few thousand miles."

The feasting and formalities went hand in hand with a practical demonstration of the white men's fire power. The expedition had taken along an air gun, capable of firing faster than any known Kentucky rifle. In addition, a swivel gun was mounted on one of the boats.

An unexpected death cast a shadow in the middle of that bright prairie summer. On August 19, Clark wrote in his journal:

*Sergeant Floyd is taken very bad with a bilious chorlick. We attempted to relieve him without success. He gets worse and we are much alarmed at his situation.*

The young man died the next day, apparently from a ruptured appendix. His friends buried him atop a high bluff which Lewis named in his memory; a stream that ran past the bluff into the Missouri was named the Floyd River. The men camped at the river's mouth that night, "after paying all honor to our deceased brother," as Clark recorded in his journal, adding sadly, "a beautiful evening."

It was the only fatality of the expedition. There had been some desertions or attempts at desertion; a few others would be punished for insubordination and sent back East. Some were to accompany the expedition only part way. But of those who finally crossed the continent, not a single man was lost.

September, with its blistering days and often chilling nights, found the Corps of Discovery in the wild country of the seven Sioux tribes. On September 25, the Corps made their first contact with the powerful Teton Sioux, who ruled the upper Missouri from their plains encampment. Lewis and Clark met the chiefs on a sand bar in the mouth of the Teton River, in what later became South Dakota.

*Met in council and after smoking Lewis proceeded to deliver a speech which we were obliged to curtail for want of a good interpreter. All our party paraded, gave a medal to the Grand Chief, called Black Buffalo. Said to be a good man. Second chief, the Partisan, bad.*

The chiefs and their young men were invited aboard to be shown "the boat, the air-gun, and such curiosities as we thought might amuse them." But the white men were just as curious about their visitors, and their notes have left us some fine descriptions of the Plains Indians at the height of their glory.

*The men shave the hair off their heads, except a small tuft on top, which they suffer to grow and wear in plaits over the shoulders. . . . In full dress, the men of consideration wear a hawk's feather or calumet feather, worked with porcupine-quills, and fastened to the top of the head, from which it falls back. The face and body are generally painted with a mixture of grease and coal.*

*Over the shoulders is a loose robe or mantle of buffalo-skin dressed white, adorned with porcupine-quills loosely fixed so as to make a jingling noise when in motion. . . .*

The expedition almost came to an abrupt end when a group of young warriors, stirred up by the Partisan, tried to seize one of the pirogues—with Captain Clark in it! The red-headed captain drew his sword "and made a signal to the boat to prepare for action." On the big boat, the swivel gun swung into position. At this point, Grand Chief Black Buffalo lived up to his reputation as a good man by ordering the young hotheads away from the pirogue. Bows were unstrung, swords sheathed, and guns lowered. Having proved their mettle, the captains were now invited to visit the Sioux village, where a dance was arranged in their honor.

*The hall or council-room was in the shape of three-quarters of a circle, covered at the top and sides with skins well dressed and sewed together. Under this shelter sat about 70 men, forming a circle round the chief, before whom were placed a Spanish flag and the one we had given them yesterday. This left a vacant circle of about six feet diameter, in which the pipe of peace was raised on two forked sticks, about six or eight inches from the ground, and under it the down of the swan was scattered.*

Speeches were made by the hosts. Then the chief, "with great solemnity," took up

*some of the most delicate parts of the dog which was cooked for the festival, and held it to the flag by way of sacrifice; this done, he held up the pipe of peace, and* first pointed it toward the heavens, then to the four quarters of the globe, then to the earth, made a short speech, lighted the pipe, and presented it to us.

They ate and smoked for an hour, as darkness fell over the prairie.

Everything was then cleared away for the dance, a large fire being made in the center of house, giving at once light and warmth to the ballroom.

The Indian music fell strangely on the white men's ears, but Lewis and Clark were fascinated by the spectacle before them.

The orchestra was composed of about ten men, who played on a sort of tambourine formed of skin stretched across a hoop, and made a jingling noise with a long stick to which the hoofs of deer and goats were hung; the third instrument was a small skin bag with pebbles in it. These, with five or six young men for the vocal part, made up the band. The women then came forward highly decorated; some with poles in their hands, on which were hung the scalps of their enemies; others with guns, spears, or different trophies, taken in war by their husbands, brothers, or connections. Having arranged themselves in two columns, one on each side of the fire, as soon as the music began they danced toward each other till they met in the center, when the rattles were shaken and they all shouted and returned back to their places.

Leave-taking was not without its difficulties, the Sioux being divided about how to treat their visitors. Fortunately for the expedition, Black Buffalo accompanied

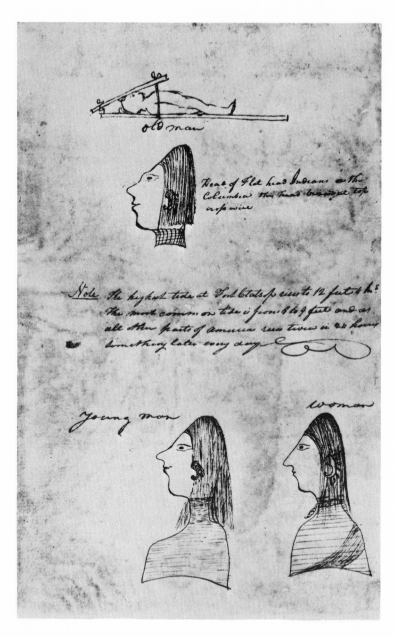

From the journals of Lewis and Clark.

them as passenger for a distance and finally departed, promising "that we would now see no more Teton, and that we might pass unmolested." Black Buffalo was as good as his word. The Teton gave them no trouble. Nor did any of the other tribes along the way to the Rockies.

The Corps continued up the Missouri, now penned in by high cliffs so curiously eroded over the centuries that Lewis thought at first they were Indian-made fortifications. The lush grasslands had the appearance of a huge wild-animal preserve, as Lewis noted in the journal.

*Great numbers of buffalo and elk on the hills, a great number of grouse. Vast herds of buffalo, deer, elk and antelope were seen feeding in every direction as far as the eye of the observer could reach. I saw several foxes.*

They first mistook the antelope for goats. The foxes turned out to be coyotes.

This was a country steeped in mysteries—mysteries that Lewis and President Jefferson had often discussed in the quiet of their evenings together in the Executive Mansion. There had been legends of a solid mountain of rock salt, of a colony of tiny people, and of a tribe of "white Indians" said to be descended from a vanished colony of Welsh settlers.

The expedition found no trace of the salt mountain. The legendary abode of the tiny people, when Lewis finally located it, was occupied by a prairie dog village. And the "white Indians" of frontier myth turned out to be the light-skinned Mandan, their hosts for the winter of 1804. Though related to the Sioux, the Mandan Indians struck Lewis and Clark as being far more agreeable; Lewis found their women "more handsome," and their men much less truculent. They lived, some twelve hundred all in all, in two villages on the upper Missouri, in huts made of bent poles daubed over with mud.

By now it was November and ice was forming on the river. The captains decided to encamp downstream from the Mandan villages for the winter. The men fell to cutting timber and building shelters, and by November 20, they were able to move into their cabins. They were just in time. "Such frost," wrote the New Englander Sergeant Ordway, "I never saw in my life!" The big thermometer a St. Louis craftsman had made for Lewis plunged below the zero mark. "The thermometer stood at 22° below," Lewis recorded. Three days later he wrote, "The mercury this morning stood at 40° below." But the men, swinging their axes in the biting cold, continued to work on the stockade, which they called Fort Mandan.

*The works consist of two rows of huts or sheds, forming an angle where they join each other; each row containing four rooms, of 14 feet square and 7 feet high, with plank ceiling, and the roof slanting so as to form a loft above the rooms, the highest part of which is 18 feet from the ground; the backs of the huts form a wall of that height, and opposite the angle the place of the wall is supplied by picketing; in the area are two rooms for stores and provisions.*

Fort Mandan was completed the day before Christmas, 1804.

In spite of the frost, it was a reasonably cozy winter. The neighboring tribes of Mandan, Minnetaree, and

Arikara came by with gifts of food and requests for assistance in hunting, healing, and even patching up family quarrels.

*We were again visited by crowds of Indians of all descriptions, who came either to trade or from mere curiosity. Among the rest Kagohami or Little Raven, brought his wife and son loaded with corn, and she then entertained us with a favorite Mandan dish, a mixture of pumpkins, beans, corn, and choke-cherries with the stones, all boiled together in a kettle, and forming a composition by no means unpalatable.*

In the evenings, the men danced to lively tunes ground out by the expedition's fiddler in residence, the boatman Peter Cruzat. The men's love of dancing was a constant source of wonder to the Indians—as was Clark's Black servant, York, who tolerantly allowed his skin to be rubbed with a wetted finger to prove "that he was not a painted white man."

Early that winter, the expedition acquired two more members from a nearby Minnetaree village: Toussaint Charbonneau, a French-Canadian trader and interpreter, and his squaw, a young captive Shoshone girl named Sacajawea. Only in her teens and due to give birth in another four months, the little Shoshone seemed a strange choice for the expedition. But her people were a Rocky Mountain tribe, and she alone, of the entire expedition, could speak their language. Little was known of the great Continental Divide that was the home of the Shoshone, but one thing was certain: the Corps of Discovery would never get across the mountains without their help.

*Indian ceremony by a Teton Dakota artist.*

On February 11, 1805, the Corps acquired its youngest member: Sacajawea gave birth to a son. "A fine boy," Lewis recorded in his journal. The baby was to accompany the expedition all the way to the Pacific and back.

The following April, "the ice having broken up," the expedition resumed its journey and its race with the seasons. They were now following the Missouri westward toward the Rockies and across what would later be Montana. The boats would have to be exchanged for horses and the mountains crossed before the onset of the next winter.

Beyond the site of modern Helena, Montana, they came to three streams—the headwaters of the Missouri. The largest of these Lewis named the Jefferson, and they followed it until they could no longer drag their craft over its shallow bed.

The Great Plains lay behind them. Soaring before them now were the mountains rising to the Continental Divide, their peaks, wrote Clark, "entirely covered with snow, white and glittering with the reflection of the sun." This was the country of the Shoshone, Sacajawea's people, who had the horses and guides needed to get the expedition through the mountains.

Contact was made with a wandering band, and Sacajawea was sent for to interpret the talk with the chief, Cameahwait.

*She came into the tent, sat down, and was beginning to interpret, when, in the person of Cameahwait, she recognized her brother. She instantly jumped up, and ran and embraced him, throwing over him her blanket,*

*and weeping profusely. The chief was himself moved,*
*though not in the same degree. After some conversation*
*between them she resumed her seat and attempted to*
*interpret for us; but her new situation seemed to over-*
*power her, and she was frequently interrupted by her*
*tears.*

Lewis and Clark got their horses. In return they bartered various items from their dwindling load of supplies. It was clear now that there was no water route through the Rockies, but Lewis had already stood on a high hilltop and caught his first glimpse of a river flowing westward. "A handsome, bold, creek of cold, clear water," he called it, and it flowed through the pass that was to lead them to the western slope of the Continental Divide.

Cameahwait had warned them of the rigors of the journey and sent guides along. They would find practically no game, he said. His own people never ventured all the way across. The only ones who did were their powerful neighbors to the west, the Nez Percé, whose warriors crossed the mountains in the late summer to hunt buffalo on the eastern prairie.

Clark would remember those September days as "the wretched portion of our journey, where hunger and cold in the most rigorous form assail the wearied traveler." Months later he wrote in his journal that "not any of us have yet forgotten our suffering in those mountains. I think it probable we never shall."

They reached the Clearwater River, the first navigable stream west of the Divide, and the first of the rivers that would lead them to the long-sought Columbia. They were descending to the high plateau between the Rockies and the Cascades, following a path that led them along the future border between Idaho and Washington.

High up in the hills above the timber line, they were exposed to snowstorms and near-starvation. "Nothing to eat but berries," wrote Clark, "our flour out, and but little corn." In the absence of game, they killed and ate an occasional colt from among their horses.

*Our guns are scarcely of any service, for there is no living creature in these mountains, except a few small pheasants, a small species of gray squirrel, and a blue bird of the vulture kind about the size of a turtle-dove or jay; even these are difficult to shoot.*

It was a half-starved, sickly group that fought its way down out of the mountains. The Indians of the plateau, particularly the powerful Flathead and Nez Percé tribes, proved friendly and sold the explorers dried salmon, roots, and berries. The sudden change from the stringent mountain diet made the party violently ill. But even in the face of hunger and disease, the Easterners still marveled at the beauty of the Northwest.

*On descending the heights of the mountains the soil becomes gradually more fertile, and the land through which we passed this evening is of an excellent quality. It has a dark gray soil, though it is very broken, with large masses of gray freestone above the ground in many places. Among the vegetable productions we distinguished the alder, honeysuckle, and huckleberry common in the United States and a species of honeysuckle known only westward of the Rocky mountains, which rises to*

*the height of about four feet and bears a white berry. . . .*
*The whole valley from these hills to the Rocky moun-*
*tains is a beautiful level country, with a rich soil covered*
*with grass. There is, however, but little timber, and the*
*ground is badly watered. The plain is so much lower*
*than the surrounding hills, or so much sheltered by*
*them, that the weather is quite warm, while the cold of*
*the mountains is extreme.*

They also marveled at the industry of the Nez Percé
Indians, who seemed like the inhabitants of a new Eden.
They were hunters, fishers, and gatherers.

*During summer and autumn they are busily occupied in*
*fishing for salmon and collecting their winter store of*
*roots. In winter they hunt the deer on snow-shoes over*
*the plains, and toward spring cross the mountains to the*
*Missouri for the purpose of trafficking for buffalo-robe.*

They were also a handsome people, living in small
semipermanent settlements on riverbanks and raising
large herds of the prized Appaloosa horses on the lush
grasslands of the high plateau. The explorers found the
Indian men "stout, portly, well-looking," and their
women "small, with good features and generally handsome." All were "fond of displaying their ornaments,"
but the men outshone the women in this respect.

*The buffalo or elk-skin robe decorated with beads; sea-*
*shells, chiefly mother-of-pearl, attached to an otter-skin*
*collar and hung in the hair, which falls in front in two*
*cues; feathers, paints of different kinds, principally*
*white, green, and light blue, all of which they find in*
*their own country; these are the chief ornaments they*
*use. In the winter they wear a short shirt of dressed*

skins, long plaited leggings and moccasins, and a plait of twisted grass around the neck.

The expedition branded their horses and promised the Indians a reward for keeping them until they returned. Then they cut down big pines growing on the hillside and hollowed them into dugouts.

On October 7, they were on their way again, fighting rapids and hidden sand bars down the Clearwater, into the Snake, and finally the Columbia.

The northwestern winter was descending, cold and damp. The morning of November 7, 1805, began in the usual dreary way, according to Clark's brief weather report: "A cloudy foggy morning. Some rain." Then the fog lifted.

*O, the joy! We are in view of the ocean, this great Pacific Ocean which we have been so long anxious to see! And the roaring or noise made by the waves breaking on the rocky shores!*

Actually, they had reached the mouth of the Columbia, so wide at this point that they could not see across. Seven more days were to pass before they arrived at "a beautiful sand beach" and had their first view of the ocean and its spray-frosted waves rolling in from faraway China.

They had crossed the great central wilderness of the American continent, the first white men to do so! This was, of course, nothing new to tribes like the Nez Percé, who frequently crossed the Rockies for hunting, but a trail had now been blazed linking the European settlements of the East and Midwest with the plains and hidden valleys of the Far West. Shorter and better routes would be found, but all would be offsprings of the tortuous path that Lewis and Clark had cut through the mountains and plains on their year-and-seven-months' journey from the mouth of the Missouri River. Other men would come for furs, then for gold, and then for the land itself.

The Corps built a log stockade on the coast and spent a cold, wet winter there, hoping that one of the ships trading along the coast would sight them. It was a vain hope. The following spring, the party broke camp and started the weary trek back overland. Ten months later, on September 23, 1806, their pirogues put in at St. Louis.

"We suffered the party to fire off their pieces as a salute to the town," Clark wrote. "We were met by all the village and received a hearty welcome." They had been given up for dead, they learned, since nothing had been heard of them since they had left Fort Mandan.

Although the people of St. Louis were used to seeing buckskins, they would long remember the appearance of these gaunt-limbed, thick-bearded men, brown as old leather, in rawhide-stitched elk and deer skins and buffalo-hide moccasins. "They really have the appearance of Robinson Crusoes," one spectator observed.

They had been away from civilization for two years and four months, and the officers in the garrison had much to tell them. The little U.S. Navy had met and conquered the Tripoli pirates of North Africa, who had been preying on American shipping. President Jefferson had been reelected to a second term, but former Vice President Aaron Burr was now a fugitive, facing a charge of high treason.

# A *La Claire Fontaine*

Two French rivermen acted as guides to the Lewis and Clark expedition. *A La Claire Fontaine* is a French love song that has been sung in the American wilderness from the time of the first settlements in the seventeenth century. It remains popular with French Canadians to this day.

À la claire fontaine
M'en allant promener,
J'ai trouvé l'eau si belle
Que je m'y suis baigné
    refrain: Lui ya longtemps que je t'aime,
        Jamais je ne t'oublierai.

J'ai trouvé l'eau si belle
Que je m'y suis baigné,
Sous les feuilles d'un chêne
Je me suis fait sécher.
   refrain

Sous les feuilles d'un chêne
Je me suis fait sécher,
Sur la plus haute branche
Le rossignol chantait.
   refrain

Sur la plus haute branche
Le rossignol chantait.
Chante, rossignol, chante,
Toi qui as le coeur gai.
   refrain

Chante, rossignol, chante,
Toi qui as le coeur gai,
Tu as le coeur à rire,
Moi je l'ai-t-à pleurer.
   refrain

Tu as le coeur à rire,
Moi je l'ai-t-à pleurer;
J'ai perdu ma maîtresse
Sans l'avoir mérité.
   refrain

J'ai perdu ma maîtresse
Sans l'avoir mérité,
Pour un bouquet de roses
Que je lui refusai.
   refrain

Pour un bouquet de roses
Que je lui refusai
Je voudrais que la rose
Fût encore au rosier.
   refrain

Je voudrais que la rose
Fût encore au rosier,
Et moi et ma maîtresse
Dans les mêm's amitiés.
   refrain

## ☆ 6 ☆

# HIGH TREASON

In February, 1807, a fugitive dressed in the rough clothes of a Mississippi riverboatman, his features almost hidden under a dirty felt hat, was arrested in a backwoods cabin some fifty miles above the settlement of Mobile, Alabama. As the prisoner was brought to nearby Fort Stoddert, it was hard to recognize the elegant New Yorker who had once been vice president of the United States.

A month earlier, on January 22, President Jefferson had informed Congress of a conspiracy "against the peace and safety of the Union," accusing Aaron Burr of being "the principal actor, *whose guilt is beyond question.*"

By the end of March, Burr was sitting in prison at Richmond, Virginia, awaiting trial for treason. There were various charges against him, including that of planning an attack on Mexico. But the most serious of these was the president's statement that Burr intended "the severance of the Union of these States by the Allegheny Mountains." It was a powerful accusation, and since it came from a powerful source, few thought to question it.

For Aaron Burr, it seemed the end of a trail that had led him first south, then west, and ultimately into hiding in the Alabama wilderness. The two and a half years that had elapsed since the encounter with Hamilton had made a wanderer of him. His house and belongings in New York were long since sold to pay his debts. Returning to Washington, he had finished his term as vice president—the murder charge applied only in New York and New Jersey—but his political career was over.

The relationship with Jefferson, never a close one, had worsened over the years—a process fed by mutual suspicion, vicious rumors repeated in the heated party press, and Burr's natural independence. In time Jefferson's feelings would harden into hatred. But in 1805 the newly re-elected president still observed a surface politeness to the man whom he feared, whom he would never understand, and whom he had rejected as his running mate the previous year.

Like many a disappointed American, Burr went west to repair his shattered fortunes. At first he received a hero's welcome. In the frontier country, there was no disgrace in killing a rival in a duel, especially a man associated with the moneyed interests of the East. Burr was feted by a succession of generous hosts, including one Harmon Blennerhassett, a wealthy Irish pioneer who had settled on an island in the Ohio River. A gentleman scholar and dabbler in science, Blennerhassett was intrigued with the possibility of fame; he put his fortune at Burr's disposal.

By 1805 the real loadstone for ambitious men lay beyond the older frontier of Kentucky and Tennessee in the

*Aaron Burr by John Vanderlyn.*

new lands of Louisiana. Burr had plans of his own for the inland empire. With Blennerhassett's money, he recruited enthusiastic young men who were ready for adventure in the new territory and possibly in Mexico. Flatboats were built and outfitted to float the men down the Ohio and Mississippi to their eventual destination.

Burr later insisted that his plan was to establish a colony of hardy young settlers on a 400,000-acre tract along the Washita River in what is now the state of Louisiana. Disputes with Spain about the southern frontier had continued in the wake of the Louisiana Purchase; they were not to be settled for another generation. In the meantime, war with Spain seemed not only possible, but very likely. Burr's projected settlement would be poised right near the border of Spanish Texas. If war developed, he did not deny that he and his colonists would be ready to invade Mexico for the United States. The notion that he plotted to annex Mexico to the West as part of a breakaway state he dismissed with disdain.

Jefferson charged that the Washita settlement was a smoke screen. "A third object was provided, merely ostensible," he told Congress,

to wit, the settlement of a pretended purchase of a tract of country on the Washita claimed by a Baron Bastrop. This was to serve as the pretext for all his [Burr's] preparations, an allurement for such followers as really wished to acquire settlement in the country and a cover under which to retreat in the event of a final discomfiture of both branches of his real design.

The charges were based on confidential reports by two prominent military men. One was Colonel George

Morgan, a veteran of the Revolution, now settled on a plantation near Pittsburgh. At the trial, Morgan was to tell how Burr tried to persuade his two sons to join in with him. The other was General James Wilkinson, governor of the Louisiana Territory, an old friend from Burr's army days, and—unknown to anyone but himself and the Spanish—an informer in the pay of Spain.

Wilkinson claimed knowledge of a plot by Burr to provoke war with Spain, invade and conquer Mexico, and combine it with the states west of the Alleghenies in a great new empire. As evidence, he had forwarded to Jefferson a letter sent to him by one of Burr's agents after the Louisiana governor had pretended to go along with the plans.

"I, Aaron Burr," the letter began, "have obtained funds and have actually commenced the enterprise." It continued:

Detachments from different points, and under different pretenses, will rendezvous on the Ohio, 1st November. Everything internal and external favors view; protection of England is secured—Navy of the United States are ready to join, and final orders are given to my friends and followers. Wilkinson shall dictate rank and promotion of his officers. Burr will proceed westward, 1st August, never more to return; with him goes his daughter; the husband will follow in October with a corps of worthies.

The letter failed to disclose Burr's ultimate aim, but it did outline a plan for transporting upwards of five hundred or one thousand men down the Ohio and the Mississippi as far as Natchez, "there to determine

*Theodosia Burr, also by Vanderlyn.*

whether it will be expedient in the first instance to seize on or pass by Baton Rouge." Baton Rouge was a Spanish settlement. To add to the mystery, the letter was written in code. Wilkinson had enclosed a translation for the president's benefit, plus a code key.

Now, in the spring of 1807, Burr's flatboat flotilla was scattered, with Burr himself awaiting trial. The plot to break up the Union, the government decided, had been hatched on Blennerhassett Island, then within the boundaries of Virginia. Burr would therefore have to be indicted and tried in the Federal Circuit Court for the District of Virginia, sitting in the little capital town of Richmond. Blennerhassett was named as his alleged coconspirator. The Federal Circuit Court judge was Cyrus Griffin, but his part in the proceedings would be of little importance. The real power was wielded by the presiding judge, Chief Justice John Marshall, Richmond's leading citizen.

Thanks to the Judiciary Act passed during the first Jefferson administration, Supreme Court judges were required to sit in on circuit court cases. For Marshall, this meant folding his tall, lanky frame into a sulky twice a year to cover the circuit courts between Richmond and Raleigh, North Carolina, a distance of 175 miles. The Burr trial, at least, would be held right at home.

It would also prove to be one of the most important trials in American history. Not only would it determine whether the fifty-one-year-old Burr must hang for high treason, it would engage the Republican President Jefferson in a dramatic, if long-distance, confrontation with his Federalist chief justice.

Richmond promptly became the most crowded community in the country. Nothing to compare with this trial had ever occurred—a former vice president facing death on the gallows for high treason. Spectators slept three and four to a bed in the town's inns and boarding-houses, camped beside their wagons in vacant lots, and argued deep into the night in the taverns.

Among the visitors was a young writer from New York named Washington Irving. To Irving, just turned twenty-four, Burr seemed like a figure out of a Greek tragedy.

*Though opposed to him in political principles, yet I consider him as a man so fallen, so shorn of power to do national injury, that I feel no sensation remaining but compassion for him. I am very much mistaken if the most underhanded and ungenerous measures have not been observed toward Colonel Burr. He, however, retains his serenity and self possession unshaken.*

The string of government witnesses had its colorful aspects. Captain William Eaton, an army officer and one-time consul to Tunisia, claimed that Burr had un-folded to him a plan for "revolutionizing the territory west of the Allegheny, establishing an independent empire there; New Orleans to be the capital, and Burr to be the chief." Burr, Eaton claimed, had sought to enlist him when the ex-consul was in Washington press-ing a $10,000 claim against the government. Eaton further described how he had shown his visitor the door in patriotic indignation. Now he paraded the streets of Richmond dressed in brightly colored, baggy North African pantaloons, a flaming-red sash, and a big, floppy desert hat.

But Burr had his defenders as well. Standing on the front stoop of a grocery store, a tall, spare visitor with graying hair told a hostile crowd, "Aaron Burr is a brave man and a patriot who wanted only to lead the Americans against the hated Spaniards." If the crowd listened, it was because General Andrew Jackson was doing the talking. A Tennessee planter and politician who had helped build flatboats for Burr, Jackson had come seven hundred miles on horseback to attend the trial.

From his Richmond lodgings, Jackson wrote a friend, "I am more convinced than ever that treason was never intended by Burr. I am sorry to say that this thing has assumed the shape of a political persecution."

In the public mind, the Burr affair had all the elements of treason and mystery: a rich immigrant, a palatial island estate isolated in the back country and therefore the perfect setting for conspiracy, seemingly endless amounts of money, and a disappointed politician known for his ambition. It seemed to be an open-and-shut case.

Burr himself remained the greatest mystery of all, understood only by one person—Theodosia. Whatever emotions Burr may have allowed himself in his desperate situation were now poured into his letters to his daughter.

*April 26, 1807*
*You have read to very little purpose if you have not remarked that such things happen in all democratic governments. Was there in Greece or Rome a man of virtue and independence, and supposed to possess great talents, who was not the object of vindictive and unrelenting persecution?*

The court convened May 22, 1807, in the hall of the House of Delegates, the largest auditorium in the town. A grand jury was impaneled to examine the facts and decide whether or not to hand down an indictment. Considering the composition of the twenty-four-man grand jury, Burr was skeptical of his chances of avoiding trial.

"Respecting the approaching investigation," he wrote to Theodosia, "I can communicate nothing new."

*The grand jury is composed of twenty democrats [a shortened form of Democrat-Republicans, as the Jeffersonians were often called] and four federalists. Among the former is W. C. Nicholas, my vindictive and avowed personal enemy—the most so that could be found in this state (Virginia). The most indefatigable industry is used by the agents of government, and they have money at command without stint. . . . The democratic papers teem with abuse against me and my counsel, and even against the chief justice. Nothing is left undone or unsaid which can tend to prejudice the public mind, and produce a conviction without evidence.*

For twenty-four days, everyone marked time waiting for General Wilkinson, the government's star witness, to arrive from the West so that his testimony could be submitted to the grand jury. Smoking was allowed in court and so was tobacco chewing, with sandboxes conveniently spotted down the aisles. The thermometer stayed above 90 degrees, and the courtroom, one sweating spectator remembered, "was hot enough to bake bread." Washington Irving wrote:

*I am impatient for the arrival of this Wilkinson, that the whole matter may be put to rest; and I never was more mistaken in my calculations, if the whole will not have a most farcical termination as it respects the charges against Colonel Burr.*

Even the presumed damning evidence of Wilkinson's letter to the president was not available to the defense. When they tried to subpoena the president along with the evidence, Jefferson scornfully replied that

*the leading principle of our Constitution is the independence of the legislative, executive and judiciary of each other. Would the executive be independent of the judiciary if it were subject to the command of the latter?*

But while a president could decline to appear, a general could not. "Wilkinson has arrived!" Irving wrote home, and he described the dramatic encounter between accuser and accused.

*Burr was seated, his back to the entrance, facing the judge, and conversing with one of his counsel. Wilkinson strutted into court and took his stand in a parallel line with Burr on his right hand. Here he stood for a moment like a turkey cock and bracing himself for the encounter of Burr's eye. The latter did not take any notice of him until the judge directed the clerk to "swear General Wilkinson"; at the mention of the name Burr turned his head, looked him full in the face and with one of his piercing regards, swept his eye over his whole person from head to foot, as if to scan its di-*

mensions, and then coolly resumed his former position and went on conversing with his counsel as tranquilly as ever. The whole look was over in an instant; but it was an admirable one. A slight expression of contempt played over his countenance, such as you show on regarding any person to whom you were indifferent, but whom you considered mean and contemptible.

General Wilkinson had an uncomfortable time before the grand jury. He was compelled to admit that he had made several deletions in decoding the cipher letter from Burr, fearing they might embarrass him. His own early willingness to go along with the alleged conspiracy was sharply questioned. But after hearing him, the grand jury indicted Burr and Blennerhassett, first, for treason "in assembling an armed force, with a design to seize the city of New Orleans, to revolutionize the territory attached to it, and to separate the western from the Atlantic states," and second, for high misdemeanor "in setting on foot, within the United States, a military expedition against the dominions of the King of Spain." Death by hanging was the penalty for the first offense, an indefinite prison term for the second.

Washington Irving returned to New York just before the trial got under way. Before leaving, he paid a last call on Aaron Burr.

He was then in the Penitentiary. Burr seemed in lower spirits than formerly; he was composed and collected as usual; but there was not the same cheerfulness that I have hitherto remarked. I bid him farewell with a heavy heart. I never felt in a more melancholy mood than *when I rode from his solitary prison. Such was the last interview I had with poor Burr, and I shall never forget it.*

In the courtroom, George Hay, the chief prosecuting attorney, acting as Jefferson's eyes and ears, watched the judge carefully as the indictment was handed down and sent his observations to Washington. Years back, Hay wrote, Marshall had told him personally that Burr was "as profligate in principle as he was desperate in fortune."

*I remember his words; they astonished me. Yet when the grand jury brought in the bill, the chief-justice gazed at him for a long time, without appearing conscious that he was doing so, with an expression of sympathy and sorrow as strong as the human countenance can exhibit without palpable emotion.*

Transferred to the penitentiary a mile and a half from Richmond, Burr tried to keep up Theodosia's spirits with a lighthearted letter.

*I have three rooms in the third story of the penitentiary, making an extent of one hundred feet. My jailer is quite a polite and civil man—altogether unlike the idea one would form of a jailer. You would have laughed to have heard our compliments the first evening.*

*"Jailer: I hope, sir, it would not be disagreeable to you if I should lock this door after dark.*

*"Burr: By no means, sir; I should prefer it, to keep out intruders.*

*"Jailer: It is our custom, sir, to extinguish all lights at nine o'clock; I hope, sir, you will have no objection to conform to that.*

"Burr: That, sir, I am sorry to say, is impossible; for I never go to bed till twelve, and always burn two candles.

"Jailer: Very well, sir, just as you please. I should have been glad if it had been otherwise; but, as you please, sir. . . ."

While I have been writing different servants have arrived with messages, notes, and inquiries, bringing oranges, lemons, pineapples, raspberries, apricots, cream, butter, ice, and some ordinary articles.

Burr urged his daughter to come to Richmond but warned, "Remember, no agitations, no complaints, no fears or anxieties on the road, or I renounce thee."

A further letter reached Theodosia on the road. "Some good-natured people" would be providing a house for her and he would be transferred back to his lawyer's house in town. In the blank space left on the letter, Theodosia noted, "Received on our approach to Richmond. How happy it made me!"

The grand jury had done its job. Now it would be up to the twelve-man petit jury to try Burr on the heavy charges laid down in the indictment. After another delay of two weeks, in which the defense tried vainly to round up some unprejudiced jurors, the trial began.

But even as the first witness was called, Burr's chief lawyers, the combative Marylander Luther Martin and the eloquent Virginian John Wickham, asked Marshall to define what evidence would be admissible. Two principles for judging treason were involved—one based on the common law of England, the other on Article III, Section 3 of the United States Constitution.

The older doctrine was that of *constructive treason,* which maintained that the accused could be linked to a crime regardless of whether he was on the scene or not. Marshall himself had applied the principle in an earlier decision that year, stating:

*If a body of men be actually assembled for the purpose of effecting by force a treasonable purpose; all those who perform any part, however minute, or however remote from the scene of the action, and who are actually leagued in the general conspiracy, are to be considered as traitors.*

It was an ancient doctrine, on the basis of which almost anyone could be connected with a conspiracy, tried, and executed. This was an evil that the writers of the Constitution had sought to avoid when they defined the crime of treason—and the proof thereof—in the most specific terms possible.

Luther Martin was a large, emotional man, given to dramatic gestures and to heavy drinking. He was also one of the finest lawyers in the country, a graduate of the Revolution and the Continental Congress, a perpetual rebel with a sensitive nose for repression either by the government or by the mob. He therefore asked that the evidence admitted be pertinent, that it be confined to what his client had *done,* rather than what he had *said.*

The judge's ruling was clear and direct: It must be proven that treason had actually been committed, that there had been an *overt act.* Mere intent to commit treason was not enough. In the case of murder, the killing must be established before other evidence was relevant; so with treason, as defined in the United States Constitution. And it must be proven by two witnesses.

In support of his ruling, Marshall quoted Article III, Section 3 of the Constitution:

*Treason against the United States, shall consist only in levying War against them, or in adhering to their Enemies, giving them Aid and Comfort. No person shall be convicted of Treason unless on the Testimony of two Witnesses of the same overt act, or on Confession in open Court.*

It was a wise and courageous decision. Only a few weeks before, the American frigate *Chesapeake* had been attacked, disabled, and boarded by the British frigate, *Leopard*, just off the coast of Virginia. Four seamen were removed to the British ship, which sailed off leaving American dead and wounded behind. The country, already aroused by accusations of treason thrown about by the administration and the Republican newspapers, seemed ready to take out its resentment on fancied traitors in its midst. Marshall, in making his ruling, had entered a brief for sanity.

The trial continued. Captain Eaton took the stand as first witness. He repeated the story of his meeting with Burr in the capital. Burr then asked him about his $10,000 claim against the government: Had it ever been paid? Eaton, under oath, said yes—after he had accused Burr of treason.

Another witness was Commodore Thomas Truxtun, a naval hero of the Revolution and the sea war with France, who had been retired after he criticized the administration's naval policy. Burr, he testified, had told him of his plan to settle the Washita tract and invade Mexico the moment a border incident provoked war with the United States. He had turned down Burr's offer to command a naval force against Mexico because the project had not been cleared with the president. Burr took up the line of questioning.

Burr: *Did you ever hear me express any intention or sentiment respecting a division of the Union?*

Truxtun: *I never heard you speak of a division of the Union.*

Burr: *Did I not state to you that the Mexican expedition would be very beneficial to this country?*

Truxtun: *You did.*

Burr: *Had you any serious doubts as to my intention to settle those lands?*

Truxtun: *So far from that, I was astonished at the intelligence of your having different views, contained in the newspapers.*

Testimony from workingmen on Blennerhassett Island disclosed little. They had prepared riverboats for the trip south. There were promises by Blennerhassett of Mexican treasure. They had seen little of Burr, who was usually downriver contracting for supplies or raising volunteers.

Colonel George Morgan and his two sons took the stand and told of Burr's visit to their plantation. The Colonel testified:

*After dinner, in the presence of a considerable company, Colonel Burr talked in a strain that shocked and troubled these good people. I spoke of our fine country. I observed that, when I first went west, there was not a single family between the Allegheny Mountains and the Ohio; and that by and by we should have Congress*

*sitting in this neighborhood of Pittsburgh.*
"No, never," said Colonel Burr, "for in less than five years you will be totally divided from the Atlantic States."

Suddenly and dramatically, the defense objected to hearing any more witnesses until the actual crime, the *overt act* of treason, was established as Justice Marshall had stipulated. Down the ages in the Old World, the defense reminded the government, men had been tortured on the rack, burned at the stake, gibbeted in chains on the mere suspicion of treasonable intentions. The framers of the Constitution had guarded against such tyranny for Americans. Where was the proof of treason accomplished or of Burr's physical presence on Blennerhassett Island when and if it was plotted there?

The motion caught the prosecution by surprise. Even their star witness, Wilkinson, who was yet to be called to the stand, could point to no overt commitment to treason in the cipher message from Burr. Moreover, Burr had never set foot on Blennerhassett Island. While Marshall, in his loose-sleeved black robe and sweat-wilted wig, listened attentively, the attorneys argued for six days, the government citing the English doctrine of constructive treason as the basis for their case.

Then, in the course of the arguments, prosecuting attorney George Hay turned his rhetoric against Marshall, warning him of possible impeachment. Burr's lawyers protested, but Marshall let the remark pass. There was a deadly political enmity between John Marshall and Thomas Jefferson. No one had to remind the Chief Justice that his fate was in the scale along with that of Aaron Burr.

Late on Saturday evening, August 29, the debate

*John Marshall by J. W. Jarvis.*

ended. For the first time in twenty-six court days, still-ness settled over the hot, smoke-clouded chamber. Marshall gathered up his notes and went home to labor over his decision. It took him two days to write it and nearly three hours to read it when court reconvened on August 31.

In a nod, perhaps, to the prosecution, the chief justice granted the difficulty of establishing treason under the restrictions of the Constitution. But at the same time, he warned, an overriding desire to win the case could result in a violation of both the letter and spirit of the law.

*If it be said that the advising or procurement of treason is a secret transaction which can scarcely ever be proved in the manner required by this opinion, the answer which will readily suggest itself is that the difficulty of proving a fact will not justify conviction without proof....*

Article III, Section 3 of the Constitution was explicit. It was formulated by men who, a generation ago, had all been traitors in the eyes of a government they regarded as despotic. Therefore, their fear of treason ran second to their fear of handing any government a statute that might be turned into an instrument of persecution.

The government had set out to prove that treason had been committed on Blennerhassett Island. A string of witnesses had testified about what Burr had written, spoken, and commissioned in numerous places in the United States. But no one man—let alone two—had actually seen Burr organize a conspiracy to commit treason, on the designated spot.

*The present indictment charges the prisoner with levying*

war against the United States, and alleges an overt act of levying war. The overt act must be proved, according to the mandates of the Constitution and of the Act of Congress, by two witnesses. It is not proved by a single witness. The presence of the accused has been stated to be an essential component part of the overt act in this indictment . . . and there is not only no witness who has proved his actual or legal presence, but the fact of his absence is not controverted. The counsel for the prosecution offer to give in evidence subsequent transactions at a different place and in a different state, in order to prove—what? The overt act laid in the indictment? That the prisoner was one of those who assembled on Blennerhassett's Island? No; that is not allowed. It is well known that such testimony is not competent to establish such a fact. The Constitution and law require that the fact should be established by two witnesses; not by the establishment of other facts from which the jury might reason to this fact. The testimony then is not relevant.

Marshall had rendered a decision that would echo in American courtrooms for generations to come. The ancient common law concept of constructive treason had been rejected in favor of the enlightened principles embodied in the Constitution. And by those lights, the government had failed to prove its case.

Returning to the prosecution's charge of his alleged "political considerations," Marshall then answered his accusers:

Much has been said in the course of the argument on points on which the court feels no inclination to comment particularly; but which may, perhaps, not improperly receive some notice.

*Statehouse, Richmond, Virginia, 1802;*
*designed by Thomas Jefferson.*

*That this court dares not usurp power is most true. That this court dares not shrink from its duty is not less true. No man is desirous of placing himself in a disagreeable situation. No man is desirous of becoming the peculiar subject of calumny. No man, might he let the bitter cup pass from him without self-reproach, would drain it to the bottom. But if he have no choice in the case, if there be no alternative presented to him but a dereliction of duty or the opprobrium of those who are denominated the world, he merits the contempt as well as the indignity of his country who can hesitate which to embrace.*

He concluded:

*The jury will apply the law to the facts, and will find a verdict of guilty or not guilty as their consciences may direct.*

The jury returned in a few hours. It declared that Burr was "not proved to be guilty under this indictment by any evidence submitted to us. We therefore find him not guilty."

Burr's neck was saved. But it was a dark victory, both for him and for Blennerhassett, who was also acquitted. They were bankrupt. The government had Burr reindicted on the misdemeanor charge in Ohio, where Marshall would not be the judge. In the meantime, Burr's creditors were closing in on him. The press and public, inflamed by the word *treason*, credited his acquittal to legal trickery. In Baltimore, where he had been greeted by cheers in 1801, a mob gathered under his window and he had to be spirited out of town. In Philadelphia, an old friend, the banker Charles Biddle, found him "concealed in a poor French boarding house, pale, dejected, alone."

Together Burr and Theodosia planned a new life for him, outside the United States. On June 7, 1808, he sailed aboard a packet for England, under the name H. E. Edwards. Theodosia had raised the money for the trip from loyal friends in New York. The English minister in Washington had indicated possible British support for a Burr expedition into Mexico that would topple the Spanish rulers there, open the country's wealth to England, and gain a throne for Burr. As the ship prepared to leave New York, father and daughter clung to each other in a last embrace. They would never see each other again.

At first Burr was confident. He was well received in London, the guest of economist Jeremy Bentham and essayist Charles Lamb. But the British government was not interested in his plans for Mexico. Months passed and his funds were running out, and Theodosia was unable to send more. Worse, she was gravely ill. Her anguished father wrote:

*O my guardian angel! Why were you obliged to abandon me just when my enfeebled nature doubly required your care? How often, when my tongue and hands tremble with disease, have I besought heaven either to reunite us or let me die at once!*

But reunion remained a far-off hope. While Theodosia tried to clear the way for his return, Burr was ordered out of England and traveled to Sweden, Denmark, and Germany. "The Grand Tour," he called it. But it was a tour of small, squalid rooms, and even these were paid for with borrowed funds. Burr's journal mirrored his despair and concern for his daughter, now back in South Carolina.

*To the watchmaker's. He has mended the hinge of the*

*case, which was worn out. Everything wears out. You will wear out. No, alas! you perish joyless in those infernal swamps. I wear out slowly. Really slowly, as you see.*

He went to France hoping to gain an audience with Napoleon. Napoleon refused to see him. Burr's money was running dangerously low:

*I have now exactly three francs, four sous; about five shillings New York money. My boots are at the shoemaker's to be soled, and I cannot redeem them.*

Burr's ambitions had shrunk considerably. All he wanted was to go home and see again his daughter and grandson. The misdemeanor charge, Theodosia wrote, would not be pressed. His creditors had also relented. But he was unable to get a passport. "A passport is all I ask," he wrote his daughter, "and thus far refused."

Not until March 27, 1812, nearly four years after he left America, was he able to sail for home. Back in New York, he opened a law office. His reputation for legal wizardry soon had clients flocking to him; the long trauma seemed ended. Then a letter came from Theodosia:

*A few miserable days past, my dear father, and your late letters would have gladdened my soul; and even now I rejoice at their contents as much as it is possible for me to rejoice at anything; but there is no more joy for me; the world is a blank. I have lost my boy. The child is gone for ever. He expired on the 30th of June.*

The death of the bright eleven-year-old, named for him, was a crushing blow to the aging Burr. But there was worse to come. Theodosia had promised to return to New York as soon as she felt well enough to travel. Her father sent a messenger to arrange her passage by sea, since he wished to spare her the rigors of a long, overland journey. A sturdy pilot boat, the *Patriot*, was engaged, and on December 30, 1812, it cleared Charleston for New York.

Two weeks later, Theodosia's husband wrote to her at her New York address, assuming she had arrived. Burr was frantic. There had been a severe storm off Cape Hatteras. He paced the Battery, New York's waterfront, his glass focused on every sail that showed on the horizon. Days passed, and weeks. Long after all reason for hope was gone, clients, seeing his office empty, knew where they could find him—alone against the sea wall, staring silently into the distance.

☆| 7 |☆

# THE BRINK OF WAR

The year 1807 brought new developments in an old war. Bonaparte, now bearing the self-assumed title of Napoleon I, Emperor of the French, stood at the height of his power. His plans for challenging England at sea had been destroyed two years before when the French and Spanish navies fell before the British fleet in the waters off Spain's Cape Trafalgar. But on land Napoleon seemed to be invincible. Since the renewal of hostilities in 1803, the French armies had swept Europe. In 1805 at the battle of Austerlitz, they defeated the combined forces of the Russian and Austrian empires. The following year, they triumphed over the Kingdom of Prussia at the old German town of Jena. Napoleon had entered Berlin in triumph, had come to an agreement with the czar, and would soon be marrying the daughter of the Austrian emperor. As 1807 opened, all of Europe, from Spain to Poland, from the North Sea to the Mediterranean, lay at the Corsican's feet.

Great Britain, across the English Channel, now found the Continent lined up against her. But she was still mistress of the seas, and now she used her fleet to blockade Napoleonic Europe. In 1806 Napoleon had enacted the Continental System, which excluded British commerce from Europe. In turn, the English Orders in Council forbade any nation from trading with countries under Napoleon's control. *Any* ship caught trading with the French, said the arrogant British, would be subject to capture and confiscation. "Every vessel," said the high-sounding Order in Council of November, 1807,

*trading from or to the said countries, together with all goods and merchandise on board, and all articles of the produce or manufacture of the said countries or colonies, shall be captured and condemned as prize of the captors. . . .*

This was a serious matter indeed. England was now claiming the right to control American shipping anywhere in the world. The fundamental issue of the freedom of the seas was thus raised. It may well be that this was one of the principal reasons why the United States went to war with England for a second time, in 1812.

Napoleon, not to be outdone by the British, answered the Order in Council with his Milan Decree of December, 1807. "Every ship," said the French emperor,

*to whatever nation it may belong, that shall have submitted to search by an English ship, or to a voyage to England . . . is thereby and for that alone, declared to be denationalized, to have forfeited the protection of its king, and to have become English property. . . . They are declared to be good and lawful prize.*

Both countries were trying to starve each other out. Both claimed the right to seize peaceable neutral shipping, to confiscate trade goods, and to interfere with the commerce of noncombatants.

But there was one thing that made British interference more odious than the French, and that was impressment. Impressment was the practice of kidnapping young men and compelling them to serve as able seamen in the British navy. This was nothing new: the navy and its press gangs had been seizing British subjects and forcing them into service for many years before the outbreak of the War of 1812—such high-handed practices had actually contributed to the outbreak of the American Revolution.

The *Lowlands of Holland,* an English song that in this form probably dates from the eighteenth century, tells of a young man actually dragged from his marriage bed to involuntary servitude.

## The Lowlands of Holland

Last Eas - ter I was mar - ried, that night I went to bed, There came a bold sea cap- tain who stood at my bed head, Say-ing a -

rise, a - rise you married man, and
come a - long with me To the
low, low-lands of Hol - land to
face your en - e - my.

Last Easter I was married, that night I went to bed,
There came a bold sea captain who stood at my bed head,
Saying, "Arise, arise, you married man, and come along with
    me
To the low, lowlands of Holland to face your enemy."

She clasped her arms about me, imploring me to stay.
Up speaks this bold sea captain, saying, "Arise and come away!
Arise, arise, you married man, and come along with me
To the low, lowlands of Holland to face your enemy."

"Oh, daughter dear, oh, daughter dear, why do you thus lament?
There are men enough in our town to make your heart content."
"There are men enough in our town, but there is not one for
    me,
For I never had but one true love and he has gone from me."

"No shoes shall come upon my feet nor comb come in my hair,
No fire bright nor candlelight shine in my chamber more;
And never will I married be until the day I die,
Since cruel seas and angry winds parted my love and me."

Now in 1807, in the great struggle with France, the navy was England's lifeline. But English sailors were deserting their warships whenever they could, many of them finding new berths on American ships, where the discipline was not so harsh and the pay was better: an American seaman might draw as much as $30 a month, while only $7 a month was doled out to his British counterpart. And His Majesty's navy sought solutions in appeals rather than improvements.

"Oh, countrymen, defenders of your country!" exhorted a handbill signed "One Old Tar" and distributed on British ships.

*Is this generous, or like yourselves? The manly zeal of the British tar stands distinguished as a sea-mark on the map of the world. In the moment of her greatest need would you desert that Sovereign Isle into whose hands has been placed the rightful sceptre of the sea, by which she is encompassed? If you persist in your rebellious measures your boasted TRUE BLOOD will be stained forever. Your mistresses will desert you, for where is the honest-hearted girl who will trust a sailor false-hearted to Old England? Your children will be ashamed to take up a profession which their fathers have disgraced! Be GOOD MEN AND TRUE SAILORS!*

But more than patriotism was needed to make up for the hardships of a sailor's life aboard a British man-of-war.

*Building a warship,*
*Philadelphia, 1800.*

So to keep her navy properly manned, England continued with impressment at sea, a policy the United States was powerless to stop, short of war. During the years between 1800 and 1810, some ten thousand American sailors were seized and forced to serve aboard British ships. The theory was that they were still British subjects owing allegiance to the British Crown.

One sailor who lived through it described the brutality of this experience. Joshua Davis had been a crewman aboard a Massachusetts ship when it was captured by a man-of-war in the North Atlantic. Davis was compelled to serve on six warships before he managed to desert and make his way home. During that time, he was confined in irons five times and flogged for minor offenses, carrying the scars on his back for the rest of his life.

Addressing "those of my countrymen who should happen to be forced on board of any of the ships of His Brittanic Majesty," he warned them first of all to abstain from drinking, and also to avoid mingling with the British crewmen.

*If you get intoxicated and fight with one of your own class, you are put in irons one night, and the next day are brought on deck, tied up to the gangway, and the boatswain's mate gives you a dozen lashes.*

*If you strike a midshipman [a junior officer] you are put in irons and receive four dozen lashes.*

*If you strike an admiral, a commodore, captain or lieutenant, you are tried by court martial and sentenced to be hung up at the yard arm or to be flogged through the fleet. You have a right to choose whether you will be hung or flogged. . . .*

The death sentence seemed almost merciful compared with flogging through the fleet, as described by Davis:

> . . . you go into the long boat with the master at arms, where you are tied up by your hands to a machine made for the purpose. The boatswain's mate comes down and gives you fifty lashes with a cat-o'-nine-tails. . . .
> In this manner you are carried from ship to ship, until you get the number of lashes imposed upon you. During this, the drummer beats the dead march, and the bell strikes half minute strokes. If you live through it, you are taken to your ship, your back washed with brine, and cured as soon as possible. But if you die before you receive the full complement you are taken to every ship and get every lash the court martial ordered. Finally you are put in a coffin, carried to low water mark and there deposited.

Stealing was punished by running the gauntlet between two rows of shipmates brandishing lengths of tarred, knotted rope.

> The boatswain starts you by a stroke on the back with his cat-o'-nine-tails. Every man then strikes you as hard and as fast as he can.
> You have to go round the deck three times in this manner. It is in vain for you to cry, scream, jump, roll, for you must bear it. Finally you look like a piece of raw beef from your neck to your waist. You are taken down to the cockpit, and there have salt brine rubbed on your back. If you are so fortunate as to get over this, you must go to work again.

For many years American diplomats had been trying,

without success, to get the British to abandon impressment.

The American frigate *Chesapeake* had sailed from Norfolk, Virginia. Barely over the horizon, she was overtaken by the British frigate *Leopard*, whose captain sent a detail aboard with a demand to search the *Chesapeake* for British deserters. James Barron, captain of the American frigate, replied that he could not permit another ship's officers to muster his crew. The detail returned to the *Leopard*, and the British frigate opened with broadsides at point-blank range.

Barron was unprepared for action. In fifteen minutes the *Chesapeake* was a wreck, her hull pierced by twenty-two round shot, her masts smashed, three of her crew killed and eighteen wounded, including Barron.

Captain Barron ordered his flag pulled down. His crew was mustered and four men were arrested as British deserters: one had enlisted under a false name, the other three were Americans who had been impressed into the British navy and escaped. The *Leopard* sailed off with the prisoners, leaving the *Chesapeake* to struggle back to Norfolk.

Barron, commodore of the Mediterranean fleet and a veteran of the Revolution, was court-martialed, convicted, and sentenced to a five-year suspension in rank and pay. He never lived down his disgrace.

President Jefferson sent a stern note to the British government demanding "honorable reparations" and disciplinary action against the commander of the *Leopard*. At the same time, he hoped to avoid war. The American navy possessed only a few ships the size of the *Chesapeake*. The army had also been pared down. At the first sign of hostility, the frontier might flare up all along the Ohio Valley and the Great Lakes.

On the other hand, the British Isles, cut off from continental Europe and more than ever dependent on America for foodstuffs and raw materials, might yield to economic pressure. On December 22, 1807, the Republican-controlled Congress obediently enacted the Embargo Act, drafted by Jefferson. The measure forbade American ships to sail to any foreign port. Coastal vessels were required to give bond double the value of ship and cargo that they would trade only with American ports. The Embargo Act spelled ruin for the very industry it was designed to protect.

Cries of anguish rose along the seaboard, particularly in maritime New England. Idle ships glutted the harbors. Waterfronts swarmed with landlocked sailors. Warehouses bulged with raw cotton, wool, indigo, and naval stores. Within the year, the value of the nation's exports fell from $108,000,000 to $22,000,000.

> Our ships all in motion once whitened the ocean,
> They sailed and returned with a cargo;
> Now doomed to decay, they have fallen a prey
> to Jefferson—worms—and Embargo.

went a popular ballad of the times. The song was first published in the *Herald* of Newburyport, a typical New England seaport near the mouth of the Merrimack River on the northeastern tip of Massachusetts. Settled 170 years earlier by English Puritans, the town had grown prosperous by shipping the farm and forest products that were floated down the Merrimack over to England and the Continent. It received European goods in exchange and played host to whaling ships. Shipyards along its sandy shores turned out schooners and seagoing sloops.

The embargo brought all this to a standstill. By April 5, 1808, the *Herald* reported:

*The following is a correct list of vessels now laying in this port embargoed: 15 ships, 27 brigs, 1 barque, 27 schooners. Total, 70 vessels.*

A week later, the fifteen ships had increased to twenty-four. Soon the *Herald* announced:

*Our wharves have now the stillness of the grave—indeed, nothing flourishes on them but vegetation.*

Sarah Ann Emery's father ran the town tavern. The farmers bringing their cattle and crops to market still needed a place to eat and sleep, so the Emerys were lucky. "Many of our neighbors," wrote Sarah in her memoirs, "had not the money to buy even a piece of meat."

*Wood was so scarce and high, that peat [dried marsh bottom] came into general use. Mr. Emery owned a peat meadow and we burned peat in all our fireplaces. It greatly surprised a young Irish peddler, who had brought a piece of his native bog in his pocket all the way from the old country, to show us as a curiosity, and to look at when homesick, never dreaming that there were peat bogs in America.*

As the ranks of the hungry and jobless increased, thievery became more common. The Emery family awoke one morning to find that

*Burglars had removed the putty from a pane of glass,*

passed in a hand and taken out the nail which fastened the window. Having made a good meal of hashed meat and bread, they took a large silver spoon, a couple of overcoats, two or three pairs of boots, some stockings and underclothing—and a Bible.

Families were breaking up. Newburyport's young men abandoned the land that could no longer provide a living for them. "We have lost many able seamen," said the Reverend Samuel Spring, "who to prevent begging and starving have shipped themselves on board foreign vessels and left the country." He went on:

The hand of poverty has struck off one hundred men from the town's list who were legal voters last year. How afflicting to them and their dear depressed families! This is but the beginning. Many who owe money cannot pay it at any rate, and others are so pressed that they discharge their debts under every disadvantage to their scanty property.

Faced with the possibility of a New England revolt, Jefferson agreed to substitute the Nonintercourse Act, which allowed American ships to resume trading with all nations except England and France. U.S. commerce could start taking on profitable risks again.

The Embargo Act had cost "Farmer Jefferson" most of his popularity in the North; but he was about to retire. The year 1808 was an election year, and Jefferson was feeling his age. At sixty-five, he looked forward to the quiet of his Virginia plantation.

The man he had chosen to succeed him did not present an impressive appearance. Washington Irving had once described James Madison as a "withered apple-john." This small, quiet Virginian, the lifelong friend of the outgoing president, was a key figure in the Republican party. For eight years, he had served as an able secretary of state, and prior to that, as Speaker of the House. In 1787 he had played a leading part in drafting the Constitution and incorporating into it the first ten amendments that made up the Bill of Rights.

Madison was elected at the height of the outcry against the embargo. The Federalist candidate, Charles C. Pinckney of South Carolina, polled only 47 electoral votes to Madison's 122. Despite the unhappiness of Federalist New England, the country at large was still strongly committed to the Republican party.

The change in administration went off smoothly. For the first time there was to be an inaugural ball, and the demand for tickets was staggering. Dolley Madison, the new First Lady, took it all in her stride. The new president might be stiff and withdrawn in public, but his wife was an outgoing, sparkling hostess. Washington might still be "an ugly duckling of a town," as one visitor described it, but the ball, held at Long's Hotel on Capitol Hill, was sure to be a brilliant affair.

And so it was. More than four hundred guests attended and Mrs. Madison "looked a queen," according to Margaret Smith, whose husband edited the official Republican newspaper of Washington, D.C.

*She had on a pale buff velvet, made plain, with a very long train, but not the least trimming, and beautiful pearl necklace, earrings and bracelets. It would be absolutely impossible for anyone to behave with more perfect propriety than she did. Unassuming dignity, sweetness, grace. . . .*

*Mr. Jefferson did not stay above two hours; he seemed in high spirits and his countenance beamed with benevolent joy. I do believe father never loved son more than he loves Mr. Madison.*

As the outgoing president arrived, he had asked another guest, "Am I too early? You must tell me how to behave, for it is more than forty years since I have been at a ball."

A few mornings later, Jefferson mounted his horse and rode off through the dawn mist drifting off the Potomac. Across the wooden bridge in Arlington, Virginia, a cartman raised his hat in awed recognition. Beyond, the red-clay country road rose and fell across rolling hills, an occasional patch of newly plowed fields intruding upon the pine slopes, a small farmhouse, a stretch of rail fence. Letting his horse set the pace, Jefferson rode, a tall, lean, gray-haired, plainly dressed horseman, through the scattered villages—Fairfax, Centerville, Manassas, Warrenton. No one he passed recognized him. While they had read his words, had voted for or against him, few of these villages had ever seen him or a likeness of him. Bearing steadily south by southwest, he reached Albemarle County by the second evening, saddle-weary but content.

The new man in the Executive Mansion remained deeply committed to Jefferson's principles, but there were new pressures on him from new forces within the party. The country had changed from the long strip of coastline and mountains remembered by Isaac Weld and Thomas Ashe. The Louisiana Purchase had more than doubled its size. Beyond the Alleghenies, the number of settlers had grown from 2,500 in 1801 to 25,000 in 1808.

Ohio was now a state, and many of its Indians retreated westward to Indiana and Illinois, only to be followed by the white settlers who continued to stream over the mountains and down through the river valleys.

In the frontier states, where all white male citizens enjoyed voting rights, a new breed of politician was emerging—tough, outspoken, resentful of the Indians, fervently nationalistic, and eager to extend the U.S. boundaries northward into Canada. In the congressional elections of 1811, the young militants—known as the war hawks —swept many of the older conservative legislators out of office. The generation that had made the Revolution was passing into history.

The new leaders were men in their early thirties who had learned the art of public persuasion in the rough school of rural politics—at country barbecues, tavern debates, rallies on town greens. John C. Calhoun of Abbeville, South Carolina, was a logician and a scholar, who at thirty could tear an opponent's argument to shreds with penetrating logic. Felix Grundy of Nashville, Tennessee, brought to Congress the alert intellect and eloquence of a successful criminal lawyer. Such men embodied the alliance between the South and the West, and the greatest of them was Henry Clay.

Clay had moved up from the Senate in an era when the main thrust of congressional power came from the House of Representatives. Like Grundy, he was a brilliant frontier lawyer. Tall, lean-bodied, careless in dress but with an inborn self-assurance, Clay possessed a flair for the dramatic that made him a commanding figure in the new Congress—especially when his fellow hawks put him in the Speaker's chair. Addressing the House, he declared:

*French wallpaper honoring Commodore Isaac Hull and commemorating the battle of the* Constitution *and the* Guerrière.

*What are we to gain by war has been emphatically asked. In reply, I would ask what are we not to lose by peace—commerce, character, a nation's best treasure, honor!*

Speaking on December 3, 1811, Clay called the financial losses caused by the British blockade "sufficient motive for war." He moved to make the impressment of American sailors a national issue.

*Not content with seizing all our property which falls within their rapacious grasp, the personal rights of our countrymen—rights which forever ought to be sacred— are trampled upon and violated.*

Clay never hurried his words. Like the ax strokes of a lumberjack; each was delivered with telling impact. His pauses were dramatic. With studied deliberation he took the little enameled gold snuffbox out of his waistcoat pocket and flicked a pinch of the spiced tobacco into his nostrils. He breathed deeply, his gray eyes studying the faces of the congressmen seated behind their flat-topped walnut desks.

*I am one who is prepared to march on the road of my duty at all hazards. The career of encroachment is never arrested by submission. When the burglar is at our door, shall we bravely sally forth and repel his felonious entrance, or meanly skulk within our castle?*

Five months later, in April, 1812, the Republicans, at a caucus dominated by the young war hawks, nominated President Madison for a second term on the platform of war with England unless she promptly revoked the

Orders in Council. Some of the war fever had rubbed off on the president. Originally, Madison had been no more anxious for war than his predecessor, but now he gauged his party's mood correctly. On June 1, 1812, having received no sign that the British intended to relent, he sent his war message to Congress—secretly.

For two weeks, a bitter debate raged behind locked doors. The New England Federalists, ruined by the Embargo Act and the Nonintercourse Act, still opposed an open break with England. The Middle Atlantic States were lukewarm. But the West and the South held the majority of seats in Congress. The Orders in Council had kept the Western states from sending their crops to foreign markets, and some Westerners were eager to move against the Indians and their British allies in Canada.

On June 18, 1812, twenty-nine years after the Treaty of Paris that had ended the wars of the Revolution, the United States once again plunged into war with Great Britain.

Congress had no way of knowing how close the British government had come to fulfilling Madison's demands. The men kidnapped from the *Chesapeake* had already been returned. On June 23, five days after the U.S. House and Senate had declared war, a new ministry in London repealed the Orders in Council. It was too late!

☆| 8 |☆

# MAKE SAIL FOR HER!

August 31, 1812, was a memorable day for Boston. A downcast spirit overhung the city of wooden houses and its waterfront crosshatched with the spars of idle ships. While the merchants in their counting houses on State Street berated "Mr. Madison's War," the general populace, whose ancestors had helped repel the British on the road from Concord and at Bunker Hill, felt their pride deeply hurt. News had just arrived of a military disaster on the frontier. General William Hull of Connecticut, on August 16, had surrendered Fort Detroit and all his forces without striking a single blow.

Now, adding to their concern, the tall masts of a warship had appeared out of the harbor mist. Through their telescopes, men on Long Wharf identified her as the forty-four-gun American frigate *Constitution*. Watching her come to anchor in the lee of one of the many little islands in the bay, they saw cannon scars on her wooden hull and tears in her rigging. It could mean only one thing—an encounter with a British man-of-war and an ignominious escape.

Next day the *Boston Gazette* blazoned a story they found hard to credit.

The United States frigate Constitution, Captain Isaac Hull, anchored yesterday in the outer harbor from a shore cruise, during which she fell in with the English frigate Guerrière, which she captured after a short but severe action. The damage sustained by the fire of the Constitution was so great that it was found impossible to take her into port, and accordingly the crew were taken out and the ship sunk.

Particulars of the action between the Constitution and the British Guerrière were communicated to the Gazette by an officer on board the Constitution.

The account, in nautical language clearly understandable to a harbor town, was apparently straight out of the *Constitution's* log.

Lat. 41,42 N, long 55,33 W. Thursday, August 20. Fresh breeze from NW and cloudy; at 2 p.m. discovered a vessel to the southward; made all sail in chase; at 3 perceived the chase to be a ship on the starboard tack close hauled to the wind; hauled S, SW; at half past 3 made the chase to be a frigate; at 4 coming up with the chase very fast; at quarter before 5, the chase laid her main topsail to the mast; took in our top gallant sails, stay sails and flying gib; took a second reef in the topsails; hauled the courses up; sent the royal yards down; and got clear for action.

Beat to quarters, on which the crew gave three cheers; at 5 the chase hoisted three English ensigns; at five minutes past 5, the enemy commenced firing; at twenty minutes past 5, set our colors, one at each masthead and one at the mizzen peak, and began firing on the enemy and continued to fire occasionally, he wearing very often and we maneuvering to close with him and avoid being raked; at 6 set the main top gallant sail, the enemy having bore up; at five minutes past 6 brought the enemy to close action, standing before the wind; at fifteen minutes past 6 the enemy's mizzen mast fell over on the starboard side; at twenty minutes past 6, finding we were drawing ahead of the enemy, luffed short round his bow to take him; at twenty-five past 6, the enemy fell on board of us, his bowsprit foul of our mizzen rigging. We prepared to board, but immediately after his fore and main masts went by the board, and it was deemed unnecessary; at thirty minutes past 6, shot ahead of the enemy, when the firing ceased on both sides, he making the signal of submission by firing a gun to leeward.

Alerted by the bells of Old South Church on Brattle Street and Christ Church of Paul Revere memory, the people rushed into the streets to collect around those fortunate enough to obtain a copy of the newspaper. When Captain Hull—a short, stocky, wind-and-sun-browned figure in navy blues—came ashore, worshipping crowds surrounded him. Never before had a British warship of the forty-nine-gun *Guerrière*'s size lost an encounter with an enemy. And an American had broken that record—a kinsman, no less, of the other Hull!

Painfully modest, Captain Hull refused to be lionized. He turned over the detailed report he had written after the engagement to a Washington courier and went back to his ship to direct its repairs. Later that day, he sent an officer ashore with a shorter account and an accompanying letter to the secretary of the navy asking that it be the one used for publication. In the light of the reception he had received, he feared the first one might sound boastful. In a laconic public statement, he declared that all credit for the victory belonged to the stout *Constitution* and its brave crew.

But the people of that day of sailing ships were not deceived. They remembered that Commodore Barron had also had a stout ship in the *Chesapeake,* and that no censure had fallen on her crew for their inglorious surrender to the British *Leopard.* From crewmen of the *Constitution* less reticent than Hull, they extracted the dramatic details of the half-hour battle in which their commander had outmaneuvered and outfought one of Britain's finest warships and reduced it to a sinking hulk.

One who had been within earshot of Hull throughout the chase and the battle was Moses Smith, a young merchant seaman who had come into Boston the year before in response to a call for volunteers to man the *Constitution* at anchor there. Captain Hull had just been given command of the proud frigate, on which he had served his apprenticeship twelve years earlier. Hull was a nephew of Gen. William Hull who had just surrendered so disgracefully at Detroit. He had fought in President Adams's undeclared sea war with France and against the Barbary corsairs in the war with Tripoli. The reputation he brought home—of a tough and capable fighting sailor—assured young Seaman Smith that life aboard the *Constitution* would not be dull.

"My station aloft was in the larboard fore yard-arm," he wrote, "and in battle I acted as sponger to gun No. 1."

The sponger's duty was to thrust a wet swab down the cannon barrel after each shot to extinguish any smoldering embers before the next powder charge was rammed home. Gun Number 1 was near the prow on the main deck. The morning of August 20, the *Constitution* was cruising off the New England coast on the watch for enemy ships. "At 10 o'clock," Smith recalled, "the lookout cried 'Sail ho!'"

"Where away?" inquired the lieutenant in command.
"Two points off the larboard, sir."
Hull had now come on deck. His first order was to a midshipman.
"Mr. German, take the glass and go aloft. See if you can make out what she is."
German was soon above us.
"What do you think?" asked Hull with animation.
"She's a great vessel, sir. Tremendous sails."
"Never mind," coolly added Hull. "You can come down, sir. Mr. Adams," addressing another officer, "call all hands. Make sail for her."
Before all hands could be called there was a general rush on deck. The word had passed like lightning from man to man. From the spar deck to the gun deck, from that to the berth deck, every man was roused and on his feet. All eyes were turned in the direction of the strange sail, and quick as thought studding-sails were out, fore and aft. The noble frigate fairly bounded over the billows, as we gave her a rap full, and spread her broad and tall wings to the gale.

It is a picture a marine artist would have gloried to preserve. The mighty three-masted frigate with tier upon tier of white canvas soaring against the clouds, decks canted with the wind, her prow cleaving a foaming furrow through the waves. Smith continued:

The stranger laid to for us. It was evident that he was an English man-of-war, of a large class, and ready for action. As we came up she began to fire. But we continued on our course, tacking and half-tacking, taking good care to avoid being raked. We came so near on one tack that an 18-pound shot struck abaft the gun to which I belonged. Splinters flew in all directions, but no one was hurt. We immediately picked up the shot and put it in the mouth of Long Tom, a large gun loose on deck—and sent it home again with our respects.

Hull was now all animation. With great energy, yet calmness of manner, he passed around among the officers and men, addressing to them words of confidence and encouragement.

"Men," he said, "now do your duty. Your officers cannot have entire command over you now. Each man must do all in his power for his country."

At this moment a man was killed on our spar deck. He fell by the side of Long Tom, and never rose again.

Hull now determined to close with the enemy.

"Sailing master, lay her along side!"

We came up into the wind in gallant style. The stars and stripes never floated more proudly then they did at that moment. All was silent beneath them, save the occasional order from an officer, or the low sound of the movement of our implements of war. Every man stood firm at his post.

"No firing at random!" Hull ordered in a subdued

tone of voice. "Let every man look well to his aim."

This was the pride of American seamen. Correctness in taking aim did more than anything else in securing our victories.

"Now close with them," he cried, raising his voice to its sternest note of command, so that it could be heard on the enemy's decks. "Along side with her, sailing master!"

A whole broadside from our guns followed this command. The Constitution shook from stem to stern. Every spar and yard was on a tremble. We instantly followed the thunder of our cannon with three loud cheers, which rang along the ship like the roar of waters, and floated away to the ears of the enemy.

When the smoke cleared away, we saw that we had cut off the mizzen mast of the Guerrière, and that her main-yard had been shot from the slings. Her mast and rigging were hanging in great confusion over her sides, and dashing against her on the waves.

This discovery was followed by cheers from the Constitution, and the cry:

"Huzza, boys! We've made a brig of her! Next time we'll make her a sloop!"

The Guerrière returned our fire with spirit—but it passed too high, and spent its force among our light spars, rigging and sails. Our fore-royal was shot away; the flag was hanging down tangled on the shivered mast in the presence of the enemy. This sight inspired one of our men, a little Irish chap named Dan Hogan, to the daring feat of nailing the standard to the masthead. He sprang into the rigging and was aloft in a moment. He was soon seen, under the fire of the enemy, at the top-mast height, clinging on with one hand, and with the other making fast the flag. The smoke curled around him as he bent to his work, but those who could see him kept cheering him through the sulphury smoke. He was soon down again, and at his station in the fight.

Several shot now entered our hull. One of the largest the enemy could command struck us, but the plank was so hard that it fell out and sank in the water. The cry arose:

"Huzza! Her sides are made of iron!"

From that circumstance the Constitution was garnished with the now familiar title, "Old Ironsides."

Soon after the battle commenced, Lieutenant Bush fell, mortally wounded. Lieutenant Morris received a wound in the chest, but he bore himself bravely through until we won the day. The braces of both ships were now shot off. The Guerrière swung round into our mizzen rigging, so that a part of her laid right over our taffrail. One could see the whites of the eyes and count the teeth of the enemy. Our stern guns were pouring in upon them, so that we raked the ship fore and aft. Every shot told well. In a few moments the foremast was gone. The great Guerrière had become a sloop. Soon after, the mainmast followed, rendering her a complete wreck.

The Guerrière suddenly dropped to the leeward and fired a gun for assistance. They tried to haul their colors down, but every man who could be seen attempting it was shot dead from the tops of the Constitution. We thought these attempts were intended to deceive us—

for we saw the men as busy as ever in continuing the action. I heard the powder boy nearest me on board the Guerrière call to another: "Work away there! Huzza! She'll soon be ours!"

The telling small-arms fire came from the crow's-nests in the mast tops of the *Constitution*, in each of which Hull had a sharpshooter stationed with six companions loading flintlocks and passing them to him as fast as he could fire. Smith went on:

As an intended insult the English had poised a puncheon of molasses on their main stay, and sent out word:

"Do give the Yankees some switchel. They will need it when they are our prisoners."

Switchel was a favorite hot-weather beverage of the Yankee farmers, made with molasses and water. For the recipe see page 174.

But we made a very different use of this molasses from what they intended. The men in the tops tapped their sweet stuff for them in a way they had little thought of. We made the decks of the Guerrière so slippery that her men could hardly stand.

The action was now nearly at a close. The firing had become less frequent on both sides. But we dared not trust the enemy. Notwithstanding his disabled condition, it was evident he would attack us again the first opportunity. His men were still numerous, his ammunition but partly spent. We sent a boat on board, but could get no satisfaction.

*Slater's cotton mill,*
*Pawtucket, Rhode Island.*

"Let's sink them!" was the cry that ran along our decks, for we felt we were deceived. At this moment Captain Dacres (James Richard Dacres, commander of the Guerrière) appeared in one of our boats and immediately surrendered himself as a prisoner of war. The delivery of his sword to Hull was a scene never to be forgotten by we who witnessed it. His first remark was:

"Captain Hull, what have you got for men?"

"Oh," replied Hull with a sly smile, "only a parcel of green bush-wackers (backwoodsmen)."

"Bush-wackers! They are more like tigers. I never saw men fight so!"

We remained by the Guerrière all night. In spite of all our efforts, she was sinking. The prisoners and wounded had been taken off. We set a slow match to her magazine (in the morning) and left her. At a distance of about three miles we hove to. One after another, as the flames advanced, came the booming of the guns. Flash followed flash. Streams of light, like lightning, ran along her sides. The grand crash came. The quarter deck, immediately over the magazine, lifted in a mass and flew in every direction. The hull parted, and sank out of sight. It was a grand and awful scene. We immediately squared away under a cloud of sail for our native land.

## Constitution and Guerrière

The Boston broadside commemorating Hull's triumph is one of the best known and remembered of the songs to which the War of 1812 gave rise. Set to the tune of a rousing English drinking song, it expresses to perfection the cocksure Yankee boastfulness of that time.

It oft-times has been told, that the Brit-ish sea-men bold Could flog the tars of France so neat and hand-y, O; But they nev-er met their match till the Yan-kees did them catch, O the Yan-kee boys for fight-ing are the dan-dy, O! (Whistle) O the Yan-kee boys for fight-ing are the dan-dy, O!

2. The *Guerrière*, a frigate bold, on the foaming ocean rolled,
   Commanded by Dacres the grandee, O;
   With as proud a British crew as a rammer ever drew,
   They could flog the tars of France so neat and handy, O!

3. Then Dacres loudly cries, "Make this Yankee ship your
      prize,
   You can do it in thirty minutes so neat and handy, O;
   Twenty-five's enough, I'm sure, and if you'll do it in a score,
   I'll treat you to a double tot of brandy, O!"

4. The British shot flew hot, which the Yankees answered not,
   'Til they got within a space they thought was handy, O;
   "Now," Hull says to his crew, "Boys, let's see what you can
      do,
   If we take this boasting Briton we're the dandy, O!"

5. The first broadside we poured swept their mainmast over-
      board,
   Which made this lofty frigate look abandoned, O;
   Then Dacres he did sigh, and to his officers did cry,
   "I did not think these Yankees were so handy, O!"

6. Our second told so well, that their fore and mizzen fell,
   Which doused the royal ensign so neat and handy, O;
   "By George!" says he, "We're done!" and they fired a lee
      gun,
   And the Yankees struck up Yankee Doodle Dandy, O!

7. Now fill your glasses full, let's drink a toast to Captain Hull,
   So merrily we'll push around the brandy, O;
   For John Bull may drink his fill, and the world say what it
      will,
   The Yankee tars for fighting are the dandy, O!

Great Britain was as dismayed over the defeat of the
*Guerrière* as America was over the news of General
Hull's surrender of Fort Detroit. "Never before in the
history of the world," wrote *The Times* of London, "did
an English frigate strike to an American. It is not merely
that an English frigate has been taken, after what we

are free to express may be called a brave resistance, but that it has been taken by a new enemy, an enemy unaccustomed to such triumphs."

From Maine to South Carolina, America toasted "Gallant Captain Hull." While little Kennebunk, far up the coast, celebrated with a cannon salute and the ringing of its meeting-house bell, the citizens of Philadelphia heaped a melting pot with silver coins to convert into "a large and elegant piece of plate." The legislatures of New York and Massachusetts sent Hull votes of thanks. New York City and Albany voted him the freedom of the city. Charleston, South Carolina, sent him an embossed silver service.

Captain Hull took his honors in stride. Any pleasure he might have derived from them was blunted by the news that his favorite brother had died in New York the very day he returned to Boston, leaving a widow to be cared for, together with the widow and three children of another brother who had died not long before. He requested release from his command so that he could see to their affairs. On September 15 in Boston harbor, he turned over the *Constitution* to Commodore William Bainbridge and soon afterward was assigned to command the defenses of New York Harbor.

But if Britain expected to see her naval supremacy quickly restored, she was badly mistaken. On October 18 the American sloop of war *Wasp* engaged and captured the British sloop *Frolic*. On December 8 the *National Intelligencer* in Washington published one of its rare extras announcing that Captain Stephen Decatur, cruising off the Madeira Islands in the frigate

*United States*, had met up with another of Britain's mighty frigates, the *Macedonian*, and beaten her into submission. And on December 29 still another British frigate, the *Java*, had the misfortune of meeting the *Constitution*, now under Commodore Bainbridge, and was savagely outgunned and captured. America's men of the sea were paying back Great Britain with a vengeance for the *Chesapeake* affair.

### SWITCHEL

New England farmers usually took their midday meal with them to the fields in summertime. It included a jug of switchel, which was anchored in a shady stream bed to keep cool. Easy to prepare and pleasantly refreshing, it is curious that the British derided it, which they did, and that it has been practically forgotten. To two quarts of water add a half-cup of molasses, three-quarter-cup of vinegar, and a half-teaspoon of ginger. Sweeten to taste with brown sugar and chill.

# ☆| ⑨ |☆

## THE BORDER WAR

Dramatic victories at sea were all very well, but if the war was to be won, it must be won by land. At first sight this might not have seemed so very hard. The Canadian frontier stretched two thousand miles through the wilderness from Halifax in the east to Michilimackinac on Lake Huron in the west, and it was largely undefended. Only a handful of British troops stood guard in a scattering of forest stockades. The British defenders, too, could get no reinforcements from Europe in the event of invasion from the United States—England had her hands full, in 1812 and 1813, fighting the armies of Napoleon.

But the fact that Canada was almost defenseless did not mean that the Americans could take it. Mr. Madison, as much as the British, faced serious military problems. Would he "go for the jugular" and attack toward Montreal? He would have to send his men by land, down the St. Lawrence Valley or over the Lake Champlain invasion route. But the government was not exactly ready for such ambitious operations. In 1812 the U.S. regular army was not much bigger than the Canadian—there were perhaps seven thousand continental troops

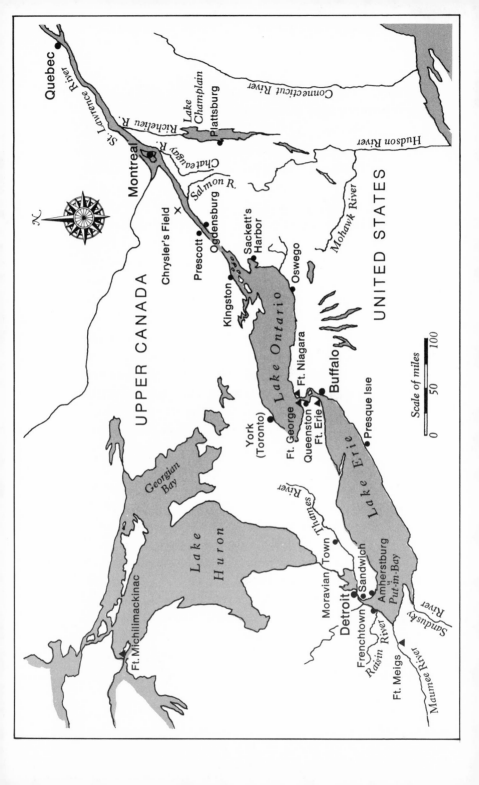

available. For a successful invasion of Canada, the militia would have to go along, too.

The militia were just ordinary people who were bound by law to take up arms to defend their homes in the event of foreign invasion, Indian uprising, or a similar emergency. That was the problem. Most militiamen, if they had spotted an invader, would not have hesitated to reach for their guns and to drive the foreigners out. This, as a matter of fact, is exactly what had happened at Lexington Green in 1775 and in many of the battles of the Revolutionary War that followed. But many militiamen, and this was particularly true in New England, felt that the federal government had no right to order them to leave home for the purpose of invading somebody else. So however much the Washington hawks wished to invade Canada, they were hindered by popular scruples on the subject. The country simply was not united behind the government's war.

It so happened that there was much more enthusiasm for an invasion of Canada in the western country beyond the Appalachians than there was in New England. Thus the first American incursion into British territory was directed against Upper Canada—the vast and beautiful wilderness area directly to the north of the Erie-Ontario waterway. In July, 1812, General William Hull left his base at the fortress of Detroit, crossed the Detroit River, and moved in the direction of the British base, Fort Malden, that lay on the other side. Capture of this stronghold was a key to the control of all Upper Canada.

By any reckoning, Hull's campaign ought to have been successful. He had a force of two thousand regulars, while his British opponent, General Isaac Brock, could only scrape together a motley band of militia and a scattering of Indians. But Hull failed miserably. He was a military holdover from the Revolutionary War, an old-timer who had become stiff in the joints and who had lost his youthful enthusiasm for the field. He was terrified of having his supply lines cut; his fertile imagination provided a hostile brave lurking behind every tree in the forest. Early in August Michilimackinac, the American outpost far to the west on Lake Huron, fell to a British attack. Hull, to the amusement of the British and the disgust of his own army, scuttled back to Detroit and bottled himself up in the fortress. This was, of course, an open invitation for the enemy to attack, and by this time Brock had organized an effective striking force. On August 15 the British forces appeared before Detroit and summoned the quavering Hull to surrender. He did so without striking a blow.

## Come All You Bold Canadians

This triumphant ballad was written to celebrate General Brock's victory over Hull.

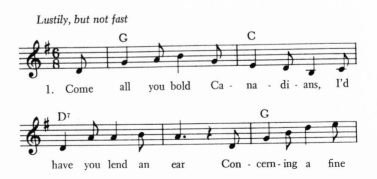

Lustily, but not fast

1. Come all you bold Ca - na - di - ans, I'd
have you lend an ear Con - cern - ing a fine

dit - ty that would make your cou - rage cheer, Con - cern - ing an en - gage - ment that we had at Sand - wich town, The cou - rage of those Yan - kee boys so late - ly we pulled down.

2. There was a bold commander, brave General Brock by name,
Took shipping at Niagara and down to York he came,
He says, "My gallant heroes, if you'll come along with me,
We'll fight those proud Yankees in the west of Canaday!"

3. 'Twas thus that we replied: "Along with you we'll go,
Our knapsacks we will shoulder without any more ado.
Our knapsacks we will shoulder and forward we will steer;
We'll fight those proud Yankees without either dread or
        fear."

4. We travelled all that night and a part of the next day,
With a determination to show them British play.
We travelled all that night and part of the next day,
With a determination to conquer or to die.

5. Our commander sent a flag to them and unto them did say:
   "Deliver up your garrison or we'll fire on you this day!"
   But they would not surrender, and chose to stand their
       ground,
   We opened up our great guns and gave them fire a round.

6. Their commander sent a flag to us, for quarter he did call.
   "Oh, hold your guns, brave British boys, for fear you slay
       us all.
   Our town you have at your command, our garrison likewise."
   They brought their guns and grounded them right down
       before our eyes.

7. And now we are all home again, each man is safe and sound.
   May the memory of this conquest all through the Province
       sound!
   Success unto our volunteers who did their rights maintain,
   And to our bold commander, brave General Brock by name!

This defeat crushed American morale. Attacks mounted that same summer against Canada on the New York frontier in the east did not help matters. So far as the invasion of Canada was concerned, 1812 ended in failure all along the line.

Thus the first year of war established the pattern of stalemate which was to be its main feature until the very end. But the whites were not the only ones whose high hopes of victory were doomed to frustration. Red Americans, too, saw in the war a means of salvation, a way to stem the tide of white settlement that was robbing them of life, liberty, and the pursuit of happiness.

The Indians of the Midwest had been traditionally allies of the British. As far back as 1763, the Crown had

A cigar-store Indian, a popular stereotype of the "first Americans;"
polychromed wood, 4′11″ high.

sought to stem the advance of colonial settlers into the Midwest, and it had used the Indians for this purpose. Fearing that continued settlement would deforest the country, destroy the fur trade, and render the colonists more difficult to control, the king had tried to limit American movement toward the west. Thus the famous Royal Proclamation of 1763 forbade the colonists from settling beyond the Appalachians, and it set up a buffer state in the Midwest which was declared to be Indian territory in perpetuity.

But the Americans didn't pay very much attention to these British orders. In the War of the Revolution, they thrust aside imperial control, took over the lands lying between the Appalachians and the Mississippi, and proceeded to settle them. Thus in the years following 1783, white settlement flowed into the Midwest. Indian power in the Mississippi Valley, all the way from the Gulf of Mexico to the Great Lakes, was faced with extinction.

In this situation there arose a young Shawnee leader who dreamed of uniting the scattered tribes and mounting a national Indian resistance to the white invasion of the western lands. His name was Tecumseh. He and his brother, known as the Prophet, traveled from the Canadian border to the Gulf of Mexico to bring their message to the red people. Tecumseh and the Prophet visited the Sauk, the Fox, the Winnebago and the Menominee of Wisconsin, the Potawatomi of Michigan, and many other tribes that hunted, fished, or farmed in the region of the Great Lakes. In the South Tecumseh visited with the Creek, the Choctaw, the Chickasaw, the Cherokee, and the Seminole. Forget your ancient differences, he said. Unite for survival.

People who were at Vincennes, capital of Indiana Territory, in 1810, remembered the tall, dignified figure of the Shawnee chief as he presented his people's case to General William Henry Harrison, governor of the territory. "Leave us our land," said Tecumseh, "leave us in peace."

*The way, and the only way to check and stop this evil, is for all the red men to unite in claiming a common and equal right in the land, as it was at first, and should be yet; for it never was divided, but belongs to all for the use of each. . . . The Great Spirit gave this great land to his red children. He placed the whites on the other side of the big water. They were not contented with their own, but came to take ours from us. They have driven us from the sea to the lakes. We can go no further.*

Tecumseh's eloquence, of course, fell upon deaf ears. The wagon trains winding through the Allegheny Mountains were getting longer every passing year; Ohio had become a state in 1803. Indiana would have enough people for statehood by 1816. What did Indian rights matter to the new settlers? "Is one of the fairest portions of the globe," as General Harrison put it,

*to remain in a state of nature, the haunt of a few wretched savages, when it seems destined, by the Creator, to give support to a large population, and to be the seat of civilization, of science, and of true religion?*

Harrison, as governor of Indiana Territory, would tolerate no opposition from the "savages" to the victorious advance of the whites and the grabbing of the

*American log house and snake fence,
by John Halkett.*

broad lands which they thought were rightfully theirs. He made the point clear by marching his troops to Tecumseh's campsite at Tippecanoe in 1811 and burning it to the ground.

Tecumseh saw that the outbreak of war between the British and the Americans provided a rare opportunity for the Indian cause. Suppose that the British were to win the war, with Indian help? The price and the reward of victory would be land for the red men and independence from the murderous interference of the Americans. Thus the war among the whites fueled the Shawnee's passionate dream of Indian unity and peace. He returned, therefore, to the ashes of his Indiana home; with burning words he rallied his followers to the support of the British. Should they, he argued, retake North America,

our rights to at least a portion of the land of our fathers would be respected by the King. If they should not win and the whole country should pass into the hands of the Long Knives—we see this plainly—it will not be many years before our last place of abode and our last hunting ground will be taken from us, and the remnants of the different tribes between the Mississippi, the Lakes, and the Ohio River will all be driven toward the setting sun.

Tecumseh and his braves joined General Isaac Brock in the first campaign of the war. Not a little of the credit for Hull's defeat, it must be said, fell to Tecumseh. On August 4 he ambushed a portion of Hull's forces at Brownstown, south of Detroit, and cut the trail upon which Hull depended for reinforcements and supplies. On August 8 Hull made a frantic attempt to reopen the road and sent out a whole battalion of men, six hundred of them, for this purpose. Again Tecumseh, with the help of a small British force, inflicted such casualties on the Americans that they withdrew to Detroit, their mission unaccomplished. And when Brock finally summoned Hull to surrender on August 15, there were as many Indians in the attacking party as there were British.

In 1813 the tide of battle in the west turned against the Crown. The capable Isaac Brock was dead, the victim of an American marksman at Queenston on Lake Ontario. He was replaced, as commander of the British forces, by the fat and lazy Colonel Henry Procter. And on the other side of the lines, a young naval officer, Oliver Hazard Perry, put in an appearance.

In the spring of 1813, Perry had been sent to Lake Erie to build a fleet and to break the British hold on that waterway, possession of which was key to the control of Upper Canada. By the first week of September, Perry was ready to join battle. The two fleets met on the lake and there was a bloody encounter; Perry's flagship the *Lawrence* was disabled. But Perry refused to accept defeat. He left his ship in a rowboat, assumed command of the *Niagara*, and continued the battle. The day's encounter resulted in the total collapse of British resistance and left the Americans in command of the lake.

With Lake Erie in American hands, Procter, who had been promoted to general, had no alternative but to evacuate his troops, stationed at Forts Malden and Detroit, and to abandon Upper Canada. There was not

Wooden bust of Commodore Perry.

much time to lose; General Harrison had already reached Detroit, and he could, if he chose, cut off the British retreat simply by ferrying troops across Lake Erie in Procter's rear.

Tecumseh received this decision with bitterness and rage. British retreat spelled the doom of the Indian cause. He confronted Procter and reproached him angrily for his cowardice. "You always told us," he said,

*to remain here and take care of our lands. It made our hearts glad to hear that was your wish. Our great father, the king, is the head, and you represent him. You always told us you would never draw your foot off British ground; but now, father, we see that you are drawing back, and we are sorry to see our father doing so without seeing the enemy. We must compare our father's conduct to a fat dog, that carries his tail on his back, but when frightened, drops it between his legs and runs off. . . . Father, you have got the arms and ammunition which our great father sent for his children. If you have any idea of going away, give them to us, and you may go and welcome. Our lives are in the hands of the great Spirit. We are determined to defend our lands, and if it be His will, we wish to leave our bones upon it.*

General Procter was in no mood to listen to Tecumseh's scornful words. By October 1, 1813, his forces were in full retreat from Malden toward the east. Ahead of them, amid tears and wailing, went the Indian women and children. With the Americans close upon his heels, Procter made a stand at Moravian Town on the Thames River. His army was routed and fled the field of battle in all directions. Only the Indian braves stood their ground, fought to the end, and died where they stood. Tecumseh was among the Indian dead.

Thus the Americans, in their turn, won control of Upper Canada—but it was to prove as flimsy and temporary a victory as the British one the year before. And as for the decisive front in Eastern Canada, the Americans in 1813 could boast of no success at all. It is true that plans were laid that summer for an invasion of Montreal, but they came to nothing. The man appointed to be the commander in chief of this ill-fated venture was General James Wilkinson, who had achieved notoriety some years before in the affair of Aaron Burr. But there was conflict among the leaders, vacillation, doubt, and endless delay. The invasion forces did not get moving until late in October; the whole operation fizzled amid the winter winds and the snow.

One and a half years of war had brought the Americans little enough success. The exception proved to be in the South. And in the first instance, the victories were scored not against the British, but against the Indians.

Before the war broke out, Tecumseh's travels, as we have seen, had taken him along the lower Mississippi and through the woodlands of Georgia and Alabama. Always the message was the same: unite against the white invader before it is too late and he has robbed you of both land and life. Tecumseh's words, it seemed, fell upon deaf ears, but with the coming of war, his work began to bear fruit. There arose a faction among the powerful Creek nation that favored resistance to the whites.

The Creek were a people who roamed the broad lands between Tennessee and the Floridas. Some of them had

*Victory parade, by an unknown artist.*

borrowed a great deal from the whites; that is, they settled down to farm the land, they adopted the Christian religion, they intermarried with the palefaces, and they even used slaves.

But not all the Creek had adopted white ways. Tilly Buttrick, who traveled their country during the war years, has left us a portrait of one of their chiefs. He was dressed, wrote Buttrick,

*in great style, with silver bands around his arms, a large silver plate on his breast, moccasins and leggings elegantly worked in Indian fashion, a handsome hat filled with plumes, with rows of beads around it, and other ornaments. . . .*

Some of these Creek chiefs favored war, and the war party were known as the Red Sticks. In the summer of 1813, the Red Sticks went on the warpath and began to attack white settlements. Terrified settlers and their families sought refuge at Fort Mims, some twenty miles north of Mobile.

On August 13, 1813, the Red Sticks stormed Fort Mims. The white settlers and their families, to the number of about three hundred people, were massacred.

Tecumseh had never ceased to warn his people against savagery of this type, and he had always urged his braves to show mercy to a defeated enemy and prisoners of war. The result of the Fort Mims massacre was to bring down upon the heads of the Creek—guilty and innocent alike—immediate white retaliation. The Tennessee militia embodied and moved down into the Creek country under the leadership of Andrew Jackson, Tennessee planter and Revolutionary War hero.

Jackson's appeal for volunteers for this punitive expedition fell upon sympathetic ears. "Brave Tennesseans!" he wrote,

your frontier is threatened with invasion by a savage foe! Already do they advance towards your frontier, with their scalping knives unsheathed, to butcher your wives, your children, and your helpless babes. Time is not to be lost. We must hasten to the frontier, or we will find it drenched in the blood of our fellow-citizens.

General Jackson was an expert at wilderness fighting; the frontier held few terrors for him. Willing recruits responded to his appeal and swelled his ranks. "Avenge Fort Mims!" was the slogan, and Indian villages were attacked and burned to the ground and their inhabitants put to the sword.

Thus did Jackson launch a systematic, pitiless war of extermination against the entire Creek nation which lasted from October, 1813, to March, 1814. The Creek braves made a desperate and tenacious resistance and lost in the process about two thousand of their best fighters. The end came at Horseshoe Bend on the Tallapoosa River in eastern Alabama. There about one thousand Red Sticks, together with their women and children, made a final stand.

Jackson attacked them on March 27, 1814, with a total force of about three thousand militia and a handful of Creek and Cherokee "friendlies." The Red Sticks were hemmed in between the encircling river and Jackson's forces. No quarter was given, and none was asked for. As Jackson himself said, "the carnage was dreadful." The Creek warriors died almost to a man; their families died with them. Only 350 prisoners were taken, and these were all women and children.

Thus whatever other results the War of 1812 had, one of them was to break Indian resistance to white advances into the broad lands stretching from the Great Lakes to the Gulf of Mexico on the eastern side of the Mississippi. Tecumseh lay dead at Moravian Town, and his vision of Indian unity died with him. The Red Stick braves lay dead at Horseshoe Bend.

The Creek and the Shawnee had fought bravely for their lives and liberties against Generals Harrison and Jackson. But in the spring of 1814, it was clear that the Americans would have to face a more formidable foe than the ragged, reluctant Canadian militiamen and the poorly armed Indian braves. That winter, 1813–14, the mighty armies of Napoleon had been crushed at Leipzig; the French emperor had abdicated his throne and had been sent into exile on the Mediterranean island of Elba. England had won her long struggle with the French, and she could now afford to give her undivided attention to the Americans.

Scarcely six weeks after the American "victory" at Horseshoe Bend, British troop transports began to cross the Atlantic headed for Quebec; in the spring of 1814, ten thousand fresh British troops arrived in Canada. They were combat-hardened veterans who had fought in Portugal under the Duke of Wellington. Proud of their record and eager for battle, they were headed for fresh and hopefully decisive offensives against the United States. The war was about to enter its most crucial phase.

☆| 10 |☆

# THE ENEMY ARE ADVANCING!

On August 16, 1814, the *National Intelligencer* of Washington, D.C., carried an alarming dispatch.

*By Express from Norfolk, 11 o'clock—A list of vessels has appeared off Rudia, 10 miles to the southward of Cape Henry* [Virginia]: *5 seventy-fours, 6 frigates, 1 sloop-of-war, 10 transports, 1 tender, a ship in the offing rating unknown.*

*1 o'clock, p.m.—Another express: the fleet have all come in from the Capes and gone up Chesapeake Bay.*

There had been talk, passed down from government circles, that the British were threatening to burn Washington in retaliation for an American raid the year before on York (now Toronto), the outpost capital of Upper Canada. Certainly the report carried in Sam Smith's *National Intelligencer* seemed to confirm that the British meant business: seventy-fours were ships of the line, and the transports were troop carriers.

However, few citizens of Washington took the report seriously. For them, as for most people on the coast, the war was a remote affair being fought out on the high seas, beyond the Alleghenies, and in the wilds of upstate

New York. Margaret Smith's optimistic letters to her sister in Philadelphia echoed the mood of the capital.

*It is generally believed impossible for the English to reach the city. There is so little apprehension of danger that not a single removal of person or goods has taken place. And our little army is full of ardor and enthusiasm. We go on regularly with our everyday occupations.*

Washington was no longer the raw little settlement that Mrs. Smith had first seen with her editor husband fourteen years before. Long rows of three- and four-story brick houses now lined the streets between the Capitol and the Executive Mansion. New fieldstone government buildings dotted Pennsylvania Avenue. But the streets were still unpaved and rutted with potholes that made carriage travel difficult after a rainstorm. To a visitor from the North, the president's house had the appearance of "a run-down Southern plantation." The grounds, enclosed in a rail fence, were covered with high grass scarred by dirt footpaths. No funds were available for upkeep.

Dispatch bearers were now galloping into the rail-fenced grounds, bringing Madison and his aides reports from the coast. Militia patrols along the Chesapeake shore had sighted the British fleet heading toward the two rivers—the Potomac and the Patuxent—that pointed their crooked fingers through the pine-fringed farmlands toward the capital.

On Saturday, August 20, the *National Intelligencer* announced:

*The latest authentic news from the enemy's fleet states that a very strong force entered the Patuxent on Thurs-*

*Paris styles, 1809.*

day and indicates an intention to ascend that river.

We have full confidence in the zeal and ability of the office to whom the protection of this district has been entrusted, and doubt not that provision has been made to meet the present crisis.

The next day, Sunday, Margaret Smith watched from her parlor window as some seven thousand militiamen marched off to confront the British, who had landed about twenty miles up the Patuxent. The citizen army, she wrote to her sister, was "composed of young mechanics and farmers, many of whom had never carried a musket." But Margaret, at least, had great faith in the commanding general, William Henry Winder.

Our troops were eager for an attack and such was the cheerful alacrity they displayed that a universal confidence reigned among the citizens and people. Few doubted our conquering.

Monday passed, then Tuesday, but on Tuesday night:

We were roused by a loud knocking. On the opening of the door, Willie Bradley called to us, "The enemy are advancing! Our own troops are giving way on all sides and are retreating to the city. Go, for God's sake, go!" He spoke in a voice of agony, and then flew to his horse and was out of sight in a moment.

By three o'clock in the morning, Mrs. Smith, her two young daughters, and her servants bundled into a carriage and set off for the village of Brookville across the Maryland border. At first it all seemed like an exciting adventure:

*The girls were quite delighted with our flight; novelty has such charms at their age. Even for myself, I felt animated, invigorated, willing to encounter any hardship.*

On Wednesday afternoon, the Smiths reached Brookville (they had stopped along the way for breakfast) and found refuge with a Quaker named Mrs. Bentley.

*Thursday: This morning on awakening we were greeted with the sad news that our city was taken, the bridges and public buildings burned, our troops flying in every direction. Our little army totally dispersed. Good God, what will be the event!*

Only one instance of heroism would be remembered from that dark Wednesday, August 24, 1814. Commodore Joshua Barney of the United States Navy, with four hundred seamen and two cannons, had contested the British advance up Chesapeake Bay. When the enemy landed, he rushed his men to the village of Bladensburg on the road to the capital and dug in across their path. There they held out until they were outflanked and overrun and Commodore Barney himself wounded and captured.

"A large part of Barney's men were tall strapping Negroes, mixed with white sailors and marines," a witness later related.

*Mr. Madison reviewed them just before the fight, and asked Commodore Barney if his "Negroes would not run on the approach of the British?"*

*"No sir," said Barney. "They don't know how to run; they will die by their guns first." They fought till a large part of them were killed or wounded.*

Paul Jennings, a Black member of the staff at the Executive Mansion, remembered that Secretary of War Armstrong "that very morning assured Mrs. Madison there was no danger."

Mrs. Madison ordered dinner to be ready at three as usual. I set the table myself. . . . While waiting, at just about three, a rider galloped up to the house, waving his hat, and cried, "Clear out! Clear out! Secretary Armstrong has ordered a retreat."

All then was confusion. Mrs. Madison ordered her carriage and passing through the dining room caught up what silver she could crowd into her old-fashioned reticule [a cloth or net handbag] and jumped into the chariot. Joe Bolin drove them over to Georgetown Heights. People were running in every direction. . . .

The British did not arrive for some hours; in the meantime, a rabble, taking advantage of the confusion, ran all over the [president's house] and stole lots of silver and whatever they could lay their hands on.

That evening, Jennings found the president and his entourage at the Georgetown Ferry waiting for the boat. They crossed together, after which "Mr. Madison and his friends wandered about for some hours, consulting what to do."

In the meantime, Mrs. Madison was looking for a place of refuge. She spent the night at one house, departed, tried another house, and found that being the First Lady had its disadvantages. The owner's wife, far from being honored, ran to the foot of the stairs and screamed, "Miss Madison! If that's you, come down and get out! Your husband has got mine out fighting, and damn you, you shan't stay in my house! So get out!"

Dolley got out. A few miles up the road, she finally found shelter.

The capital was ablaze, against the background of a fearful electric storm. Robert Gleig, a subaltern in the British army, later described the destruction.

*The flames of lightning seemed to vie in brilliancy with the flames which burst from the roofs of burning houses, while the thunder drowned the noise of crumbling walls and was only interrupted by the occasional roar of cannon and large depots of gunpowder....*

*The consternation of the inhabitants was complete.... The first impulse of course tempted them to fly, and the streets were in consequence crowded with soldiers and senators, men, women, and children, horses, carriages, and carts loaded with household furniture, all hastening towards a wooden bridge which crosses the Potomac. The confusion thus occasioned was terrible.*

Gleig went on to tell of a "detachment sent out to destroy Mr. Madison's house." On entering, they found the table still spread for Dolley's three o'clock dinner.

*They sat down to it, therefore, not indeed in the most orderly manner, but with countenances which would not have disgraced a party of aldermen at a civic feast.*

After the uninvited guests had eaten and "partaken

freely of the wines, they finished by setting fire to the house which had so liberally entertained them." By daybreak, Gleig noted, "everything marked out for destruction was already consumed."

*Of the senate house, the President's palace, the barracks, the dockyards, etc., nothing could be seen except heaps of smoking ruins.*

On Thursday violent winds and rain struck the city, uprooting trees and drenching the smoldering buildings and invaders alike. Having avenged the burning of York and shown that even the U.S. capital was theirs for the taking, the British returned to their ships and sailed for their next objective—Baltimore.

Over in Maryland, William Henry Winder, the general who couldn't save Washington, collected his scattered forces. "He appeared to regret very much that he had not been enabled to have made a greater resistance," reported a correspondent of the *Baltimore Patriot.* The midsummer temperature had soared into the nineties and the raw recruits were suffering from heat and neglect.

*The uncertainty on which road the enemy intended to attack the city compelled him to keep his forces divided, and their being divided occasioned frequent marches and countermarches, which at this hot season was quite too much for our militia, particularly as the officers were unable to procure supplies; for our men suffered severely not only for accommodations but for bread and meat.*

When the enemy troops landed on the riverbank below Baltimore during the night of September 11, they found

Winder and his Washington militiamen lined up to meet them. There were also brigades from Baltimore and the surrounding countryside. Hezekiah Niles was on the scene and described it for the readers of his *Weekly Register*.

*Their ships had ranged themselves in a formidable line to cannonade the fort and the town. The force that landed consisted of 9,000—5,000 soldiers, 2,000 marines and 2,000 sailors. They were allowed to march four miles forward uninterrupted. Then the artillery and infantry met them. The carnage was great.*
*The battle raged all day, the American forces slowly pulling back toward the town in good order. The British were allowed to get within two miles of the city, where General Winder with the Virginia militia and a squadron of cavalry planned to cut them off. The British suspected their design and decamped suddenly in the night and embarked with precipitation.*

Frustrated on land, the British concentrated on the bombardment of Fort McHenry, at the harbor's entrance. "The attack was terribly grand and magnificent," Niles wrote. But after a nightlong attack, "the enemy precipitately retired. Never was the mortification of an invader more complete." One week later an account of this action against the fort was published in a Baltimore newspaper. It was a poem by a young lawyer, Francis Scott Key, which began:

*Oh say, can you see by the dawn's early light*
*What so proudly we hailed at the twilight's last gleaming. . . .*

The day that the redcoat army marched on Baltimore

*Napoleon Bonaparte returning to France in 1814 after his exile on the island of Elba.*

some 10,000 troops moved by ship down the St. Croix River toward Lake Champlain. Their goal was the Hudson Valley, following the classic invasion route which General Burgoyne had taken in 1777.

At first resistance was easily overcome. But at the town of Plattsburgh on the lake's western shore, Sir George Prevost, governor of Canada and commander of the invading army, caught sight of a ridge "crowned with three strong redoubts and other field works, and blockhouses armed with heavy ordnance, with their flotilla at anchor out of gunshot from the shore." Within those works, fifteen hundred American regulars and a few thousand militiamen awaited the attack.

The American flotilla, commanded by thirty-year-old Captain Thomas Macdonough, lay anchored across Plattsburgh Bay. The two fleets met and a murderous engagement followed, as they exchanged broadside for broadside within pistol shot of each other. The battle lasted for two and a half hours. When it was over, the British ships had struck their flags in surrender. The following day Prevost retreated hastily to Canada.

The British thrust from the north had failed. But a greater danger threatened in the deep South. In the summer of 1814, a large force of British veterans—combat-hardened troops from England's grueling Spanish campaign—had been sent to Jamaica, there to remain poised for an attack on the American mainland. At their head was Sir Edward Pakenham, brother-in-law of the Duke of Wellington and one of England's ablest generals. Before the year was out, Pakenham and his army were sailing northward through the Gulf of Mexico, heading for New Orleans and the Mississippi Valley.

# Johnny Bull, My Jo, John

"Johnny Bull" began life as a broadside ballad shortly
after the termination of the War of 1812. We may think
of it as a brilliant recapitulation of the war from the
American viewpoint; it stresses the American national
achievement, puts the best face possible on disgraceful
episodes like the British occupation of Washington, D.C.,
in 1813, and quietly omits any reference to the less glorious
aspects of the military effort.

O, John - ny Bull, my jo John, I
won - der what you mean; Are you on for - eign
con - quest bent, or what am - bi - tious scheme? Now
list to broth - er Jon - a - than, your
fruit - less plans fore - go, Re - main on your fast -
an - chored isle, O John - ny Bull, my jo.

O Johnny Bull, my jo, John, don't come across the main;
Our fathers bled and suffered, John, our freedom to maintain,
And him who in the cradle, John, repelled the ruthless foe,
Provoke not when to manhood grown, O Johnny Bull, my jo.

O Johnny Bull, my jo, John, on Erie's distant shores,
See how the battle rages, and loud the cannon roars;
But Perry taught our seamen to crush the assailing foe,
He met and made them ours, O Johnny Bull, my jo.

What though at Washington a base marauding band,
Our monuments of art, John, destroyed with ruthless hand?
It was a savage warfare, beneath a generous foe,
And brings the more disgrace on you, O Johnny Bull my jo.

O Johnny Bull my jo, John, when all your schemes have failed,
To wipe away the stigmas, John, for New Orleans you sailed;
Far heavier woes await thee John, for Jackson meets the foe,
Whose name and fame's immortal, O Johnny Bull, my jo.

Your schemes to gather laurels here I guess were badly planned;
We have whipped you on the ocean, jo, we have bothered you
    on land:
Then hie thee to old England, John, thy fruitless plans forego,
And haste to thy fast-anchored isle, O Johnny Bull, my jo.

☆| 0️⃣ |☆

# LIKE A SEA OF BLOOD

*When the smoke had cleared away and we could obtain a fair view of the field, it looked at first glance like a sea of blood. It was not blood itself which gave it this appearance, but the red coats in which the British soldiers were dressed. Straight out before our position the field was entirely covered with prostrate bodies.*

The writer was a member of the Kentucky militia; the scene, a battlefield beside the wide, muddy Mississippi River four miles below New Orleans; the time, Sunday morning, January 8, 1815.

Behind the Kentuckian peering through the lifting black-powder smoke moved the tall, emaciated general who had accomplished this, the most spectacular American victory of the War of 1812. General Andrew Jackson had spent the night prowling the long line of breastworks confronting the British army of war-seasoned infantrymen, marines, and sailors poised to repeat the easy conquest of Washington four months before. Racked with dysentery, his left shoulder still inflamed from a bullet wound received in a tavern brawl, he had seemed to be everywhere at once—now afoot, now on horseback, counseling his officers, inspecting the artillery embrasures, or exchanging greetings with old friends among the western militiamen.

Described by a New Orleans hostess as "a tall, gaunt man, very erect, with a countenance furrowed by care and anxiety," Jackson had arrived in late November, 1814, to prepare the local defenses against a probable British invasion. Jackson, then in his forty-seventh year, was too ill to eat the elaborate Creole breakfast that his hostess had prepared for him, and his appearance, at first glance, seemed neglected.

*His dress was simple and nearly threadbare. A well-worn leather cap protected his head, and a short Spanish coat of old blue cloth his body, whilst his high boots, whose vast tops swayed uneasily around his bony knees, were long innocent of polish or blackening. His complexion was sallow and unhealthy, his long hair iron gray, and his body thin and emaciated like that of one who had just recovered from a lingering sickness. A fierce glare shone in his bright and hawk-like eyes.*

That fierceness had broken the power of the Creek Indians and brought the Tennessean overall command of the U.S. defenses in the South. Jackson had been called to the defense of New Orleans at the request of its citizens and of James Monroe, who had replaced John Armstrong as secretary of war. News of the British invasion force poised in Jamaica had already leaked to the mainland. The city was sadly unprepared. The waterways that were its lifeblood in peacetime now provided easy access for an invader. Yet no American naval force patrolled them. Except for a gunboat flotilla, qualified only to sound an

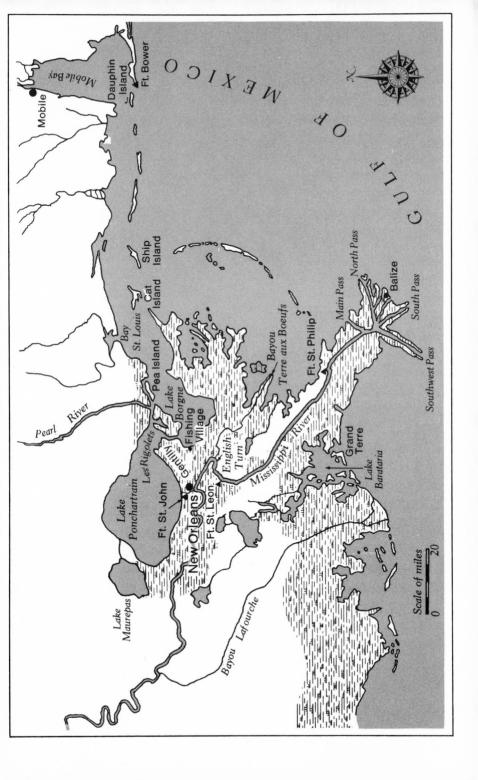

alarm, the lakes and bayous of the Mississippi Delta lay open to the enemy fleet.

In New York, the Federalist *Evening Post* pinned the blame on the Republican government.

*As predicted long since by the Federalists on the floor of Congress, the enemy has sent a force to New Orleans which, I think, according to Mr. Jefferson's definition of it, will be found to be "competent," that is to say "considerable" at least. This is another proof, if another were wanting, of the utter want of capacity in the administration, to conduct a war. . . . They seem not to have one thought of this all important point; which if it falls into the hands of the enemy, threatens us with a long-protracted war, and in all probability will be followed by a division of the empire. The western states will be dependent on whatever power holds New Orleans, the key of the Mississippi.*

The editorial was run January 8, 1815. Due to the slowness of the mail service, the *Post* had no way of knowing that Jackson's victory, falling on that very day, had already handed that key to the United States.

In the meantime, northern businessmen lived off the ancient dispatches and sweated over the fate of their goods sitting in New Orleans warehouses, an easy prey.

"We are still in a state of suspense as to the fate of New Orleans," wailed the *Post*.

*Three mails are due, which in the minds of many augurs ill. The vast amount of cotton stored in that city, a great part of which is owned by merchants in this section of the country, creates unusual anxiety. It is computed that there are upward of 100,000 bales at and in the neighborhood of that place, worth on the spot, even at war prices, upwards of a million of dollars. In Europe at the prices last quoted, it would be worth four millions. The quantity or amount of tobacco, and other staple commodities of the country stored there, we can form no estimate of. Report states it to be very large.*

Jackson wasn't thinking of the cotton bales—except perhaps for shoring up the barricades. Never one to waste time, he soon had the local militia units active again and awaited reinforcements from Kentucky and Tennessee. It was a motley army: there were Creole planters, fashionably military in their colorful uniforms, buckskin-clad frontiersmen, Santo Domingo blacks who had fought under Toussaint L'Ouverture.

Jackson himself faced some hard guesswork about the possible invasion routes the enemy might follow. To the northeast, separated from New Orleans by a narrow neck of land, lay Lake Borgne, a salty, island-dotted extension of the Mississippi Sound that brought the Gulf of Mexico almost to the back door of the city. Narrow channels carried its waters into Lake Pontchartrain farther to the west. Both tidal lakes were shallow and unfit for the transportation of troop ships beyond a given point. An invading force, Jackson reasoned, would have to land somewhere along the lakeshore, move inland to the Mississippi, and use the riverbank as a parade ground for a march on the town.

Another possible invasion route was the river itself— an enemy force might try to sail up the Mississippi. Jackson had already reinforced Fort St. Philip, guarding the mouth of the river. In the end, everything would depend on how soon Cochrane's fleet could be spotted.

On December 14, 1814, the British, hoping to stage a surprise attack, caught Jackson's little gunboat fleet at the entrance to Lake Borgne. "Great consternation prevailed," reported the *Post's* correspondent, who cited a letter received from the beleaguered city.

*We are all in confusion here. The British have taken five of the gun-boats, and the other two vessels are destroyed. . . . They are off here it is said with 40 or 50 sail, prepared with such craft as will answer to enter the Lakes and attack that way, or to come up the River, having it is said about eight thousand men on board. . . . The inhabitants of this place appear willing to a man to fight, but the militia are not numerous. . . .*

Jackson immediately placed the town under martial law.

*No persons shall be permitted to leave the city without a permission in writing signed by the General or one of his Staff.*
*No vessels, boats, or other craft will be permitted to leave New Orleans or Bayou St. John without a passport in writing from the General or one of his Staff, or the Commander of the Naval Forces of the U. States on this station. . . .*
*The Street lamps shall be extinguished at the hour of nine at night, after which time persons of every description found in the streets or not at their respective homes, without permission in writing as aforesaid, and not having the countersign, shall be apprehended as spies and held for examination.*

The measures, though harsh, matched the gravity of the

situation. Nevertheless, on December 17, "T. Johnson, Esq., Postmaster at New Orleans" wrote to the postmaster general in Washington in an optimistic mood.

All here have full confidence in Gen. Jackson and calculate on a favorable result.
Our present force is 4000 regulars and militia. To this we may add, by Sunday, 2000 Tennessee troops, under Gen. Coffee. . . . The fleet is the same that you had in the Chesapeake, and is under Admiral Cochrane. Gen. Jackson has established the most perfect order and police. He is confident he can defend the place—the accounts of the enemy's force are various. . . . Our fate will be decided before you hear from me again.

In the end, Jackson was able to face the invaders with almost six thousand men.

The enemy now controlled the tidal lakes. But where would they land? And when?

On Christmas Eve, the correspondent for the *Philadelphia Gazette* dashed off an excited letter to his paper.

I have now to inform you that at 1 o'clock yesterday, intelligence was received that a landing had been effected on the shore of Lake Borgne, and that they had penetrated to the Mississippi, at a distance of about six miles below the town; the alarm was given, and before five o'clock Gen. Jackson, with a chosen corps of about two thousand men, left the town to meet them, and at seven an action commenced and lasted scarcely two hours, terminating in the retreat of the enemy to the woods. . . .

A Creole planter had brought the word to Jackson. Trapped at first in his house by the quietly advancing British army, he had managed to escape amid a hail of

*A view of New Orleans.*

bullets, reaching New Orleans by boat and horseback. Once the news was out, Jackson wasted no time in attacking. The correspondent of the *Philadelphia Gazette* reported:

*The enemy were taken by surprise; they were encamped for the night, and were at supper when the action commenced on our part. . . . From the Government House where I am posted, I could distinctly see the fire, and the import of the guns has, as you may suppose created a great alarm among the inhabitants. . . .*
*Six o'clock—The day is breaking and we are in anxious expectation of hearing it ushered in by the sound of our artillery.*

The battle continued until Jackson, galloping from outpost to outpost, learned that the main British force had come out of the cypress swamps beyond the riverbanks. He called off the attack, leaving the British to count their dead and wounded, and withdrew.

It was all deeply disturbing to young Lieutenant George Greig of the 85th Regiment of light infantry, who had served in the assault on Washington and Baltimore. Earlier, as the advance column settled down beside the Mississippi, he had assured his friend, Captain Charles Groy, fresh from the European theater, that

*Americans never have been known to attack. We need hardly expect them to do it now.*

After the assault, he searched for his friend and found him lying beside a haystack, his head shattered.

Under Jackson's directions, the Americans withdrew northwards to a plantation between the river and the cypress swamp four miles below the city. There they fell to digging entrenchments and artillery embrasures directly across the enemy's path.

Jackson sent urgent messages calling in the units that had been guarding the other approaches to New Orleans. Soon he had 4,698 men behind the main defenses on the eastern shore of the Mississippi. The sod embankment protected men of every description: uniformed regulars and militiamen, men from the drill companies of New Orleans, riflemen from Tennessee and Kentucky, troops from Georgia, even pirates from the local jails. The variety of company commanders ran the gamut from Jackson's leathery frontier colleagues to the French-speaking officers of the local units. There were also twenty pieces of artillery.

Another eight hundred men waited on the narrower western bank of the Mississippi. But Jackson believed—and rightly—that the main British thrust would come on the broad eastern shore.

Major General Sir Edward Pakenham could not know that he faced a fighting general unlike any the Americans had produced in the war so far. Camped downriver, he posted pickets against further surprises while he organized for the frontal assault that would surely make short work of the motley collection of Americans and their upstart frontier commander. He had eleven thousand troops, men who had fought the great Napoleon to a finish. Now he waited only for the heavy naval guns to be brought across Lake Borgne to where they could fire into the American lines at point-blank range.

The Mississippi itself had prepared the battleground—a brown, barren alluvial plain, fringed on either side by cypress swamps and bisected by the winding river. Beyond the next bend, four miles upstream, was New Orleans. And on either side of the river, strung out in a line of resistance from east to west, the Americans waited behind their earthworks.

At dawn on the morning of January 8, a signal rocket flared above the British camp, splashing long trailers of light into the thick mist from the river. Bugles sounded. The British artillery opened a barrage of round shot and grape. Standing on a parapet in the middle of his earthwork defenses, Jackson saw the redcoats in their broad ranks emerging from the fog. With a hunter's practiced eyes, he watched the lines approach. Satisfied, he stepped down from the parapet and spoke to his officers.

"They're near enough now, gentlemen."

The order went up and down the embankment: "Fire!"

Sergeant John Spencer Cooper of the 7th Royal Fusiliers was a survivor of that day: he never forgot the effects of that first burst of fire.

*The two lines approached the ditch [the American earthworks] under a murderous discharge of musketry. But crossing the ditch and scaling the parapets were found impossible without ladders. These had been prepared, but the regiment that should have carried them left them behind, thereby causing, in a few minutes, a dreadful loss of men and officers.*

The lieutenant colonel assigned to provide the ladders for the assault had failed in his duty and was later cashiered out of the army.

*The front lines now fell into great confusion and retreated* behind us, leaving numerous killed and wounded. We then advanced to within musket shot, but the balls flew so thickly that we were ordered to lay down to avoid the shower.

Just before the order to lay down, my right-hand man recieved a bullet in his forehead and fell dead across my feet. Another about ten or twelve files on my right, was smashed to pieces by a cannon ball. Another had his arm near the shoulder so badly fractured that it was out of the cup. The enemy kept pounding away at us all day, during which a shower of grape came whizzing like a flock of partridges.

A member of the Kentucky militia was stationed at the left end of the American line. His letter home, written after the battle, is preserved by the Louisiana Historical Society.

Col. Smiley from Bardstown, was the first one who gave us orders to fire from our part of the line; and then, I reckon, there was a pretty considerable. There was also brass pieces on our right, the noisiest kind of varmints, that began blazing away as hard as they could, while the heavy cannon toward the river and some thousands of small arms joined in the chorus and made the ground shake under our feet.

Directly after the firing began Capt. Patterson, I think he was from Knox County, Kentucky, but an Irishman born, came running along. He jumped up on the breastwork and, stooping a moment to look through the darkness as well as he could, he shouted with a broad North of Ireland brogue, "Shoot low, boys! Shoot low! Rake them! Rake them! They're coming on all fours!"

It was so dark that little could be seen until just about the time the battle ceased. The morning had dawned, to be sure, but the smoke was so thick that everything seemed to be covered up in it. Our men did not seem to apprehend any danger, but would load and fire as fast as they could, talking, swearing and joking all the time. All ranks and sections were soon broken up. After the first shot everyone loaded and banged away on his own hook. . . .

At one time I noticed, a little to our right, a curious kind of chap known among the men as "Sukey," standing coolly on the top of the breastworks and peering into the darkness for something to shoot at. The balls were whistling around him as thick as hail, and Col. Slaughter ordered him to come down. The colonel told him he was exposing himself too much. Sukey turned around, holding up the flat of his broad-brimmed hat with one hand to see who was speaking to him, and replied:

"Oh, never mind, Colonel. I don't want to waste my powder, and I'd like to know how I can shoot until I see something." Pretty soon after Sukey got his eye on a red coat and took deliberate aim, fired, and then coolly came down to load again.

The merciless fire cut down Pakenham and most of his staff officers. Crack regiments, the pride of the British army, either died together making their way across the plain or broke up and retreated. The first prisoners came straggling in and minor acts of mercy stood out amidst the carnage. A young British soldier, "very neatly dressed," and no more than nineteen or twenty years old, needed help in getting over the breastwork to surrender to the

Americans. The anonymous Kentuckian offered his hand and "he jumped down quite lightly."

*As soon as he got down he began trying to take off his cartouche box, and then I noticed a red spot of blood on his clean white under jacket. I asked him if he was wounded, and he said that he was, and he feared pretty badly. He begged us not to take his canteen, which contained his water. We told him we did not wish to take anything but what was in his way and cumbersome to him. Just then one of the Tennesseans, who had run down to the river as soon as the firing ceased, for water, came along with some in a tin coffee pot. The wounded man asked if he would please give him a drop. "Oh, yes," said the Tennessean. "I will treat you to anything I've got."*
*The young man took the coffee pot and swallowed two or three mouthfuls from the spout. He then handed back the pot, and in an instant we observed him sinking backwards. We eased him down against the side of a tent, when he gave two or three gasps and was dead. He had been shot through the breast.*

Hours before, the Americans, spoiling for a fight, had been cheered when the British columns first approached. Most of them had never seen so impressive a sight as the red-clad regiments approaching in the early morning mist. Now a different scene met their eyes.

*Straight before our position the field was entirely covered with prostrate bodies. About two hundred yards off, lay a large dapple-gray horse, which we understood to be Pakenham's. About half way between the body of the horse and our breastwork there was a large pile of dead, and at this spot, as I was aftward told, Pakenham had been killed,* his horse having staggered off to a considerable distance before he fell.

When we first got a fair view of the field in front, individuals could be seen in every possible attitude. Some lay quite dead, others wounded, pitching and tumbling about in the agony of death. Some had their heads shot off, some their legs, some their arms.

The letter concluded:

The field . . . looked at first glance like a sea of blood. . . .

The remnants of the British force retired to their camp. General Jackson sent off a letter to James Monroe.

Early on the morning of the 8th, the enemy having been actively employed the two preceding days in making preparations for a storm, advanced in two strong columns on my right and left. They were received, however, with a firmness which, it seems, they little expected, and one which defeated all their hopes. When all prospect of success became hopeless, they fled in confusion from the field, leaving it covered with their dead and wounded. Their loss was immense.

The British had lost 2,057 killed, wounded, and missing. Of the Americans, only 21 had been killed and 58 wounded. Even worse was the fact that the British casualties included 3 major generals, 8 colonels, 6 majors, 18 captains, and 54 lieutenants.

For ten days, the two armies lay behind their defenses. Then on January 19, Jackson sent a second letter to Monroe, beginning, "Last night at 12 o'clock the enemy precipitately decamped and returned to their boats."

# The Hunters of Kentucky

The ballad reproduced here is a masterpiece of understatement which gives little hint of the grimness of the engagement at New Orleans. But as a serious account of the experience from the viewpoint of the victor, it is not very far from the truth. Men who had survived the inconceivable hardships and horrors of Wellington's Peninsular campaign were broken by the small arms fire of the Tennessee and Kentucky militia.

You gen - tle - men and la - dies fair, who grace this fa - mous cit - y, Just lis - ten if you've time to spare, whilst I re - hearse a dit - ty; And for an op - por - tu - ni - ty, con - ceive your - selves quite luck - y, For

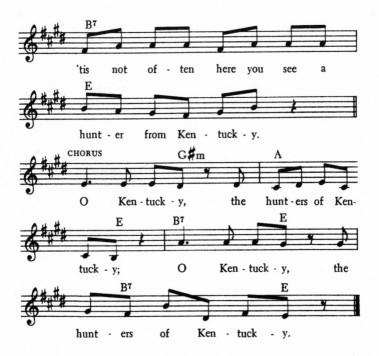

'tis not of - ten here you see a
hunt - er from Ken - tuck - y.

CHORUS

O Ken - tuck - y, the hunt - ers of Ken-
tuck - y; O Ken - tuck - y, the
hunt - ers of Ken - tuck - y.

2. We are a hardy freeborn race, each man to fear a stanger,
  Whate'er the game we join the chase, despising toil and
    danger;
  And if a daring foe annoys, whatever his strength and
    forces,
  We'll show him that Kentucky boys are "alligator horses."
  O Kentucky, etc.

3. I suppose you've read it in the prints, how Pakenham
    attempted
  To make old Hickory Jackson wince, but soon his schemes
    repented,
  For we with rifles ready cocked, thought such occasion lucky,
  And soon around the hero flocked the hunters of Kentucky,
    O Kentucky, etc.

4. You've heard I suppose how New Orleans is famed for
   wealth and beauty.
   There's girls of every hue it seems, from snowy white to sooty,
   So Pakenham he made his brag, if he in fight was lucky,
   He'd have their girls and cotton bags in spite of old
   Kentucky,
   O Kentucky, etc.

5. But Jackson he was wide awake, and wasn't scared at trifles,
   For well he knew what aim we'd take with our Kentucky
   rifles;
   So he led us down to Cypress swamp, the ground was low
   and mucky,
   There stood John Bull in martial pomp, and here was old
   Kentucky,
   O Kentucky, etc.

6. A bank was raised to hide our breast, not that we thought of
   dying,
   But that we always like to rest, unless the game is flying:
   Behind it stood our little force: none wished it to be greater,
   For every man was half a horse, and half an alligator,
   O Kentucky, etc.

7. They did not let our patience tire before they showed
   their faces—
   We did not choose to waste our fire, but snugly kept our
   places;
   And when so near to see them wink, we thought 'twas time
   to stop 'em;
   And 'twould have done you good, I think, to see Kentuckians
   drop 'em.
   O Kentucky, etc.

8. They found at last 'twas vain to fight when lead was all
   their booty,
   And so they wisely took flight, and left us all our beauty,

And now if danger e'er annoys, remember what our trade is,
Just send for us Kentucky boys, and we'll protect you, ladies,
   O Kentucky, etc.

So slowly did news travel that it was a month before the East coast learned of Jackson's victory. The February 18 issue of *Niles Weekly Register* carried the headline: GLORIOUS NEWS! The heading beneath it was a double-barreled sensation:

Orleans saved and peace<br>concluded.

"The matters detailed and recorded in the present number of the *Register* are of incalculable importance," wrote editor Niles.

*The enemy has retired in disgrace from New Orleans, and peace was signed at Ghent on the 24th of December, on honorable terms. The British sloop-of-war Favorite arrived at New York on Saturday last—passengers Mr. Carrol, one of the secretaries to our ministers at Ghent, and Mr. Baker, sent to the British legation to the United States; the former with a copy of the Treaty of Peace concluded and signed by the British commissioners at Ghent on the 24th of December, and the latter with the same ratified by the Prince Regent, and which being approved by the President and Senate, is immediately to be communicated to the British fleets and armies in this quarter of the globe.*

The Battle of New Orleans had been fought sixteen days after the war ended! The British ministers at Ghent had signed the treaty, confident that Pakenham would bring them New Orleans as a fringe benefit. But they had guessed wrongly.

## ☆| 12 |☆

# PEACE

*The British delegates very civilly asked us to dinner. The roast beef and plum pudding was from England, and everybody drank everybody else's health. The band played first GOD SAVE THE KING to the toast of the King, and YANKEE DOODLE, to the toast of the President. Congratulations on all sides and a general atmosphere of serenity; it was a scene to be remembered.*

A young American named James Gallatin made that entry in his diary on Christmas Day, 1814. Thousands of miles away on the Mississippi Delta, British and American soldiers shivered in the December rain and prepared for combat. But in the ancient Belgian city of Ghent, British and American diplomats sat side by side and celebrated the peace treaty that had been signed the day before.

The alert teenager who watched the proceedings was the son of Secretary of the Treasury Albert Gallatin, senior member of the American delegation. Although officially his father's secretary, young Gallatin felt self-conscious in that august company. He was probably wearing his Sunday best, described in his diary as

*a suit of Chinese nankeen [cotton], white silk stockings,*

*high white choker, with a breast-pin of seed-pearls mother gave me before I left home. They call my hair auburn— I call it red.*

The scene around that dinner table capped four months of wrangling between the two delegations and sometimes between the American ministers themselves. Of the five-man U.S. commission, three would have been outstanding in any age. Short, balding John Quincy Adams, son of the second president, had been his country's minister to the great courts of Europe. He was a New England man, scholarly and austere, with an eye out for the preservation of his section's fishing privileges in the waters of northeastern Canada. Henry Clay, young and combative, representing the West, bristled at British demands for navigation rights on the Mississippi. In the middle stood James's father—Swiss-born, reserved, and a man of cool judgment. If Albert Gallatin was the senior member of the delegation, Adams was the experienced diplomat. But harmony was seldom the rule, as noted by the seventeen-year-old James.

*July 14*
*Nothing to do. Mr. Adams in a very bad temper. Mr. Clay annoys him. Father pours oil on the troubled waters. I am now reading a history of the Low Countries. . . .*

And again on August 10:

*Clay uses strong language to Adams, and Adams returns the compliment. Father looks calmly on with a twinkle in his eye. Today there was a severe storm, and father said, "Gentlemen, gentlemen, we must remain united or we will fail. . . ."*

There was good reason for Gallatin's admonition, the British had the upper hand in that summer of 1814. Bonaparte, defeated, had been exiled to the island of Elba. On the high seas, three great fleets were carrying fresh British troops toward Canada, Chesapeake Bay, and the Gulf of Mexico. By the end of the year, the American coastal cities might be in ruins, New England cut off from the rest of the country, and Old England in final control of the Mississippi.

The British position was correspondingly tough, therefore, when the commissioners finally sat down to talk on August 8. That evening, James Gallatin noted in his diary:

*The British Commissioners, as a base of discussion re the treaty—demanded that the Indian tribes should have the whole of the North-Western Territory. This comprises the States of Michigan, Wisconsin, and Illinois—four-fifths of Indiana and the third of Ohio. That an Indian sovereignty should be constituted under the guarantee of Great Britain: this is to protect Canada. Father mildly suggested that there were more than a hundred thousand American citizens settled in these States and territories. The answer was: "They must look after themselves."*

To the Indians, the buffer state would spell security. Up to this point, they were the ones who had had to look after themselves. To the Americans, it meant moving the northern border of the country down from the Great Lakes to the banks of the Ohio River. The British also demanded parts of Maine and control of the Great Lakes.

"But all this means the dismemberment of the United States," James complained to his diary.

*Early nineteenth century playing cards. Shown on the cards are (clockwise) Thomas Jefferson, Andrew Jackson, John Quincy Adams, and George Washington.*

As demands and counterdemands flew back and forth across the conference table, the ostensible causes of the war—impressment and the freedom of the seas—were never even mentioned. The point was not lost on John Quincy Adams, who saw a continuation of the battles his father had fought while negotiating the treaty that ended the Revolutionary War.

"I am called to support the same interests," he wrote to the elder Adams back home in Quincy,

and in many respects, the same identical points and questions. The causes in which the present war originated, and for which it was on our part waged will scarce form the most insignificant item in the Negotiations for Peace. It is not impressment and unalienable allegiance, blockades and orders in Council, colonial trade and maritime rights, nor belligerent and neutral collisions of any kind that form the subjects of our discussions. It is the boundary, the fisheries, and the Indian savages.

For better or worse, the principles of the Treaty of 1783 were being put to the test and Adams, an old hand at international diplomacy, recognized it at once. In the meantime, the British delegates, dependent on London for instructions, stalled for time and awaited news of victory. By mid-August, James quoted a "private note" his father had written to Secretary of War Monroe:

We will not remain here long, the position is untenable; I am preparing for departure. Our negotiations may be considered at an end. Great Britain wants war in order to cripple us; she wants aggrandisement at our expense. I do not expect to be longer than three months in Europe.

In October, London received news of the British defeat

on Lake Champlain. The invasion from Canada had failed, just as the American invasion into Canada had failed two years before. The burning of Washington remained a dramatic gesture, since the British had failed to follow it up with the capture of Baltimore. Another possibility—that of sending the great Wellington over to North America as Commander—was ruled out by Wellington himself. For as the two Gallatins found out months later,

*it was the intention of the British Government to send the Duke of Wellington to America, during the Ghent negotiations, to terminate the war. It seems he refused to go, giving his reason that he could not be spared, and at the same time expressing his displeasure. . . . It seems it was mainly due to him that the English made the concessions they did and brought the matter to a speedy termination. . . .*

According to James, Wellington had already written secretly to the elder Gallatin during the negotiations. "I have only just seen it," the boy noted in his diary.

*It is marked "strictly confidential." It is couched in the most friendly terms, assuring father he has brought all his weight to bear to ensure peace. . . . Father burnt this dispatch and does not even know that I have recorded it. I wanted to copy it, and was doing so when he took it off the table and burned it.*

Even with the prospects of a victory at New Orleans, the British government could no longer afford to hold up a peace treaty. Once again, the state of affairs on the Continent had a direct bearing on U.S.-British relations

—except that this time, the effect was to end a war instead of start one. In London, Lord Liverpool, the English prime minister, advised his foreign minister that the government had decided "not to continue the war for the purpose of obtaining or securing any acquisition of territory." The British would therefore back down from their claims. Citing "the unsatisfactory state of the negotiations at Vienna," "the alarming situation of the interior of France," and "the state of our finances," Liverpool concluded:

Under such circumstances, it has appeared to us desirable to bring the American war if possible to a conclusion.

On December 24, 1814, James Gallatin could finally record in his diary:

The treaty was signed today in the refectory of the monastery. Later on there was a solemn service in the cathedral; it was most impressive. We all attended as well as the Intendant, all the officers, and the high officials of Ghent.

After the Christmas Day banquet, the boy who had seen history being made noted hopefully:

God grant there may be always peace between the two nations. I never saw father so cheerful; he was in high spirits, and his witty conversation was much appreciated.

There were no dramatic concessions, but no humiliations, on either side. The treaty gave virtually nothing to either country that it hadn't had before. Great Britain dropped her earlier demand for control of the Great Lakes and free access to the Mississippi River. Territories taken by either side were restored to their original owners. Commissioners were to settle the disputed northern border of Michigan Territory, and the question of the Maine boundary would be settled sometime in the future, too. Fishing rights were not even mentioned. The Indian state became a dead letter and the Indians remained a forgotten people.

But Britain refused to discuss the two main issues that had caused the war: impressment of American seamen and the rights of neutral shipping in wartime. America did not insist. It was equally weary of the war.

The treaty was sent off to London for ratification by the Prince Regent, ruling in place of the now-insane George III. On January 8, as the cream of the British army was being destroyed before New Orleans, James Gallatin noted:

*The ratification of the treaty completed today. A great banquet offered by the town of Ghent takes place tonight. Poor father is not looking forward to it. . . .*

On February 17, 1815, the United States Senate advised and consented to ratification, and the treaty was proclaimed the next day. News of Jackson's victory and of the treaty had arrived within the same four days. Both were greeted with relief and rejoicing.

In Washington, amid smoke-blackened ruins, cannons roared, church bells rang out, militiamen back from Baltimore paraded on Pennsylvania Avenue. "Peace! Peace!" people shouted at each other, and "Jackson! Good old Jackson!"

# CONCLUSION

Thomas Jefferson had, when he was president, a vision of the American future which was well expressed in his 1800 campaign song, "Jefferson and Liberty." The American people, removed from the squalid militarism of the Old World, would live in peace; they would be independent farmers, not grimy proletarians; above all they would be free of the bondage and the blight of slavery.

How rapidly, in the few years from 1800 to 1814, was the bubble pricked! Industrial revolution and urbanization took root in the North; a period of peace ended with a second bloody war for independence; the ominous shadow of slavery did not diminish but began to grow and spread. In these few years, the foundations were laid not only for an American industrial empire, but for a slavery empire as well. North and South, free section and slave, were set upon a collision course which would determine the destinies of the American people for years to come. For many Americans there would be no freedom, and for none would there be any peace.

In the Jeffersonian period both French and British dreams of winning back the vast inland empire of Louisiana were brought finally to an end. By 1814 the

American nation had come into firm possession of a veritable empire of land, the illimitable Mississippi Valley as far west as the Rockies. American psychology soon came to reflect this fact. Americans possessed a boundless confidence and pride in national resources and the national future, a surging vitality, a sense of the vastness of their land and life.

White Americans moved west with a confidence of success. They would cut the trees down; they would conquer the land; they would take possession of it and make it their own. But this white dream spelled the doom of the red dream. Among many visions of the American future which were fashioned in those days, the vision of Tecumseh possessed unequaled grandeur and dignity: red men, living in brotherhood and peace, would enjoy for all time the splendor of the American land and the folkways of their fathers. This dream was shattered by the white man with his guns, his blasphemous, grove-cutting axes, and his greed.

The War of 1812 was no mere incident in the period. It capped and confirmed the main thrust of social development. The war broke the power of the Indian peoples between the Appalachians and the Mississippi; it thus removed the final obstacle to American exploitation of this area and speeded up the advance into it of the free farmer and the slaveholder alike. The war shattered a formidable British invasion, and at the battle of New Orleans, destroyed forever British ambitions to control the continent. The war produced a spiraling demand for guns and clothing, speeding the growth of industry in the urban centers of the North.

Isaac Weld, the Irish traveler, packed his bags in 1801 and headed for home. But in the following years, his countrymen continued by the thousands to land upon American shores. The vision of America as a land of opportunity burned brightly in the minds of the European poor. Was this not, of all the kingdoms of the earth, the place where a poor man had the best chance to enjoy plenty and to live in peace?

*Sign from a New England tavern.*

# SONG NOTES

*Charlotte*, or *The Frozen Girl*, has been found with only minor variations in many parts of the country. The melody given here was taken by Carl Sandburg from Dr. James L. Himrod of Chicago, and published in *The American Songbag* (New York: Harcourt Brace and Co., 1927).

*John, John* is a worship song from St. Simons Island as recorded by Lydia Parrish and published in *Slave Songs of the Georgia Sea Islands* (New York: Farrar and Straus, 1942).

*Lowlands* is by origin an English ballad of great age and beauty. Some time after the Revolution it reached Black dock workers and sailors in the Gulf ports and became, in the form given here, a favorite capstan shanty.

*A La Claire Fontaine* is a traditional French song which has long enjoyed popularity among French Canadians.

*Lowlands of Holland* became a favorite song in both Britain and the American colonies during the eighteenth century. The version given here was taken by Alan Lomax from Mrs. Carrie Grover of Gorham, Maine.

*Constitution and Guerrière* is a broadside ballad composed in Boston to commemorate Hull's victory over Dacres. The melody is that of an old English drinking song.

*Come All You Bold Canadians* celebrates Brock's victory over Hull at Detroit. The song has remained popular for more than a century among Canadian woodsmen. It is taken from Fowke, Mills, and Blume, *Canada's Story in Song* (Toronto: W. J. Gage).

*Johnny Bull, My Jo, John* started life as a broadside ballad. It is an apt summary of American successes in the war, and tactfully plays down the failures. The version given here is taken from John Anthony Scott, *The Ballad of America* (New York: Bantam Pathfinder, 1964).

*The Hunters of Kentucky* brilliantly summarizes the British-American struggle for New Orleans. The ballad became one of Andrew Jackson's campaign songs and had some share in winning for him victory in the presidential campaign of 1828.

# BIBLIOGRAPHY

All books listed are in print at time of writing unless otherwise specified. * denotes paperback edition.

*General*
Henry Adams, *History of the United States during the Administrations of Jefferson and Madison,* originally published 1889–91, remains the fundamental source for this period. The complete nine-volume set has been reissued by Hilary House publishers, New York. Two abridged editions are available in paperback (University of Chicago, 1967, ed. Ernest Samuels; and Prentice-Hall, 1963, ed. George Dangerfield and Otey M. Scruggs). John Allen Krout and Dixon Ryan Fox, *The Completion of Independence* (New York: Macmillan, 1944) is a well-written modern survey of the period in the *History of American Life* series. For the Indian peoples with whom the story is directly concerned, there are two admirable references and introductory studies: * Alvin M. Josephy, Jr., *The Indian Heritage of America* (New York: Alfred A. Knopf, 1968), and * Olivia Vlahos, *New World Beginnings: Indian Cultures in the Americas* (New York: Viking Press, 1970).

*The United States in 1800*
Isaac Weld's *Travels Through the United States of North America,* long out of print, has been made available again in a modern edition (4th edition 1807, reissued by Augustus M.

Kelley, New York, 1970, 2 vols.). Timothy Dwight, *Travels in New England and New York*, first published in 1821–22, is a source of great value for this period. A fine modern edition of this work is now available (Cambridge, Mass.: Harvard University Press, 1969, ed. Barbara M. Solomon and Patricia M. King). Another source of first rate significance and great charm is Julian Ursyn Niemcewicz, *Under Their Vine and Fig Tree: Travels through America in 1797–99, 1805* (Newark, N.J.: New Jersey Historical Society, 1965, translated and edited by Metchie J. E. Budka). Highly recommended secondary sources that shed light on popular life of the time are: * J. E. Wright and Doris S. Corbett, *Pioneer Life in Western Pennsylvania* (Pittsburgh: University of Pittsburgh Press, 1968); and J. R. Dolan, *The Yankee Peddlers of Early America: An Affectionate History of Life and Commerce in the Developing Colonies and the Young Republic* (New York: Clarkson N. Potter, 1964), which, unfortunately, is now out of print.

### The Hamilton-Burr Feud

Biographies of both Hamilton and Burr have been written by * Nathan Schachner (New York: Thomas Yoseloff, 1957; and Cranbury, N.J.: A. S. Barnes, 1957, paperback) respectively. Aaron Burr's *Private Journal* has been reissued in a reprint edition (Upper Saddle River, N.J.: Gregg publishers, 1970, 2 vols.). The voluminous *Papers of Alexander Hamilton*, which ought to be available in high-school libraries, have at the time of writing been issued only to 1794 (New York: Columbia University Press, 1961–69, 15 vols., ed. Harold Syrett).

### North and South

For the great inventions and inventors of this period see * Jeannette Mirsky and Alan Nevins. *The World of Eli Whitney* (New York: Collier Books, 1952); * Roger Burlingame, *March of the Iron Men* (New York: Grosset and Dunlap, 1960; and * James Thomas Flexner, *Inventors in Action: The Story of the Steamboat* (New York: Collier Books, 1962). Steam power itself, which was just beginning to revolutionize economic production, is dealt with by * Ivor Hart, *James Watt and His Steam Power* (New York: Collier and Macmillan, 1961). Frances Ann Kemble, *Journal of a Residence on a Georgia Plantation* is a fine source for a cotton plantation that came into full production during this period (New York: Alfred A. Knopf, 1961, ed. John Anthony Scott); * C. Peter Magrath, *Fletcher vs. Peck* (New York: Norton, 1967), reveals the impact upon land values produced by the invention of the cotton gin.

### The Louisiana Purchase (two chapters)

* *The History of the Lewis and Clarke Expedition* is available in a Dover edition, 3 vols., ed. Elliot Coues. For the Plains Indians * Robert Lowie, *Indians of the Plains* (New York: Natural History Press, 1963) is an admirable introductory survey. Further fascinating detail is provided by the following (more-or-less) contemporary accounts: Washington Irving, *A Tour on the Prairies* (New York: Pantheon Books, 1967). Irving made his tour of the western prairies in 1832; and Lewis Henry Morgan, *The Indian Journals 1859–82* (Ann Arbor: University of Michigan Press, 1959). Morgan, one of the greatest of American anthropologists, gives a careful and vivid picture of Indian life; the work is profusely illustrated with drawings and paintings by contemporary artists. Further illustrations of Plains Indians will be found in Harold McCracken's magnificent *George Catlin and the Old Frontier: A Biography and A Picture Gallery of the Dean of Indian Painters* (New York: Dial Press, 1959). For full detail on the encounter with the Nez Perces, see Alvin Josephy, Jr., *The Nez Perces Indians* (New Haven: Yale University Press, 1965).

### The Burr Conspiracy

See the Schachner biography, cited above, and Thomas Abernethy, *The Burr Conspiracy* (New York: Oxford University Press, 1954). There is an excellent brief coverage in another out-of-print work, Albert J. Beveridge, *Life of John Marshall*

(Boston: Houghton Mifflin, 1916–1919) vol. III. Jonathan Daniels, *Ordeal of Ambition* (New York: Doubleday & Co., Inc., 1970) is a lively examination of Burr's relations with Hamilton and Jefferson.

## The Brink of War

The Washington Scene during the Jefferson administration is recorded in the correspondence of Margaret Bayard Smith, published recently under the title *First Forty Years of Washington Society* (New York: Frederick Ungar Publishing Co., 1965, ed. Gaillard Hunt). * James Sterling Young, *The Washington Community*, 1800–28 is a thorough study of the Jefferson establishment (New York: Columbia University Press, 1966). The diplomatic history of this period is dealt with in the detailed but masterly work by * Bradford Perkins, *Prologue to War*, 1805–12 (Berkeley: University of California Press, 1968). The question of impressment is handled by James F. Zimmerman, *Impressment of American Seamen* (1925. Reissued by Kennikat Press, Port Washington, L.I., 1966).

Biographies of Jefferson are as thick as leaves; most of them are remarkably dull. Perhaps the best introduction to Jefferson is to read what he himself wrote about his beloved Virginia. We highly recommend his *Notes on the State of Virginia* (Chapel Hill: University of North Carolina Press, 1955. ed. William Peden). As Mr. Peden points out "it is recognized today as the best single statement of Jefferson's principles."

## The War of 1812

The causes of the war of 1812 are explored in * George Rogers Taylor, ed. *The War of 1812* (New York: Heath and Co., 1963); Julius Pratt, *Expansionists of 1812* (New York: Macmillan, 1925); A. L. Burt, *The United States, Great Britain and British North America* (New Haven: Yale University Press, 1940); and * Reginal Horsman, *The Causes of the War of 1812* (New York: A. S. Barnes, 1962). Two first-rate histories of the war which, unfortunately, are now out of print are Frances

F. Beirne, *The War of 1812* (New York: Dutton) and Glenn Tucker, *Poltroons and Patriots* (Indianapolis: Bobbs Merrill, 1954, 2 vols.). There is a chapter on Tecumseh in Alvin Josephy, *The Patriot Chiefs: A Chronicle of American Indian Leadership* (New York: Viking Press, 1961). There are two recent and important studies of the New Orleans campaign: Charles B. Brooks, *The Siege of New Orleans* (Seattle: University of Washington Press, 1961), and Wilburt S. Brown, *The Amphibious Campaign for West Florida and Louisiana 1814–15* (University of Alabama: University Press, 1969). There is an excellent little study on the Battle of Horseshoe Bend in paperback, James W. Holland, *Andrew Jackson and the Creek War* (University of Alabama: University of Alabama Press, 1968).

# ACKNOWLEDGMENTS

*I would like especially to thank my editor, Miss Ann Sperber, for the meticulous care and enthusiasm with which she helped to prepare this manuscript for the press.*

*Grateful Acknowledgment is made for the use of illustrations:*

Abby Aldrich Rockefeller Folk Art Collection, 203; Arents' Collection, New York Public Library, 68; Bernice Chrysler and Edgar William Garbisch Collection, 190; Cooper-Hewitt Museum of Decorative Arts and Design, Smithsonian Institution, 157; Historical Society of York County, Pennsylvania, 9; *History of the U.S. Capitol.* Glenn Brown, 48; Hudson's Bay Company, 184; I. N. Phelps Stokes Collection, New York Public Library, 13,18,147; Index of American Design, National Gallery, 236; John Anthony Scott, 54: Kennedy Galleries, 214 Library of Congress, 35, 44, 80; Mansell Collection, 84; The Mariners Museum, 187; *Memoirs of Samuel Slater,* 169; Metropolitan Museum of Art, 64; Missouri Historical Society, 102; New-York Historical Society 21,36,37,97,118,121,196; New York Public Library, Rare Books Division, 94,229; New York State Historical Association, 181; Philadelphia Museum of Art, 6; Smithsonian Institution, 106; U.S. Patent Office, 59; Virginia State Library, 137; White House Collection, 134. The maps in this book are by Edward Malsberg.

# INDEX

LEONARD FALKNER has written a number of books about the early decades of American history, including *Forge of Liberty: The Dramatic Opening of the American Revolution* and, most recently, *John Adams: Reluctant Patriot of the Revolution.*

Mr. Falkner was born in Cleveland, Ohio, attended Ohio State University, and has had a long career as a writer and editor. He has worked on the staffs of *The American Magazine*, the *New York World-Telegram*, and the *New York World-Telegram and Sun*, where he was features editor until 1965. His articles have appeared in *American Heritage, Redbook*, and *Reader's Digest*. One of these, "George Washington's Unknown Spy," has since been reprinted in two books and six languages. Mr. Falkner and his wife live in New York City.

JOHN ANTHONY SCOTT has taught at Columbia and Amherst colleges, and since 1951 has been Chairman of the Department of History at the Fieldston School, New York. He is currently Professor of Legal History at Rutgers University. Among the many books he has authored or edited are *The Ballad of America, The Diary of the American Revolution*, and *Trumpet of a Prophecy.*

*Text set in Electra*
*Printed and bound by Jenkins-Universal Corporation, N.Y., N.Y.*
*Series styled by Atha Tehon*
*This book designed by Barbara Bert*